TO ANN

Generative

Grammar,

Structural

Linguistics,

and

Language

Teaching

NEWBURY HOUSE PUBLISHERS   ROWLEY, MASSACHUSETTS

NEWBURY HOUSE PUBLISHERS, INC.

LANGUAGE SCIENCE
LANGUAGE TEACHING
LANGUAGE LEARNING

68 Middle Road, Rowley, Massachusetts 01969

Copyright © 1971 by Newbury House Publishers. All rights reserved. No part of this publication may be reproduced in any form without permission from the publisher.

Library of Congress Catalogue Number: 73-151244

ISBN: 912066-22-9

Printed in the United States of America.   First Printing October 1971

GENERATIVE GRAMMAR,
STRUCTURAL LINGUISTICS,
AND
LANGUAGE TEACHING

PREFACE

The idea for this book dates back to 1963-64 when I was studying under that professional skeptic and critic John B. Carroll at the Harvard Graduate School of Education. Every Tuesday and Thursday during the fall term we examined research reports of people who tried to quantify and measure various language phenomena—and we found that every single report had some flaw, either technical or conceptual, which vitiated its results to some degree. It was a devastating way to begin graduate study. At the same time, I took half my courses in linguistic theory at M.I.T. under Morris Halle and Noam Chomsky—an equally revolutionary experience from a positive point of view. These three men have had the most influence in the development of my thought.

I spent the next three years earning my Ph.D. in the Harvard Department of Linguistics, and I wish to thank Karl Teeter and Calvert Watkins, chairmen of the department, for their help in broadening the scope of my study.

My Ph.D. thesis (1967) was the first draft of the material presented here. The writing of the thesis was done with the supervision of Wayne O'Neil, Einar Haugen, and Dwight Bolinger. All three are strong in their own opinions, and at least two of them were not to be easily convinced by my position. The long discussions which ensued were without question the high point of my doctoral program.

The present book is almost entirely rewritten. J. K. Galbraith recommends locking a new manuscript into a bank vault for a couple of years before revising it for publication. He was forced to do that with *The New Industrial State* when he went off to be ambassador to India. My reasons for delay are not so glorious, but I, too, recommend the practice.

The reader will soon be aware of my bias. I am critical of the theories and teaching methods which have been held by the linquistic establishment for the last several decades—the empiricist-behaviorist theory of language learning and the "audio-lingual" method of mimicry, memorization, and pattern drill. I favor the rationalist theory of language learning as put forth by Noam Chomsky, and the tightly organized direct methods of language teaching which have been based on older versions of the same theory. Sol Saporta (1966) saw that generative grammar has undermined the behavioristic theories and methods of language teaching which linguists have been recommending, but he and others in the profession have not seen what the positive contributions of generative grammar might be. This book can be seen as a statement of the implications which generative grammar should have for language teaching.

Karl Conrad Diller

CONTENTS

PART IV   CONCLUSIONS

PART I

INTRODUCTION

CHAPTER 1

THE DUAL HISTORY OF
FOREIGN LANGUAGE TEACHING

The history of foreign language teaching often appears to have been a history of failure. Not many students of foreign languages ever attain full bilingual proficiency. In fact, very few language majors in American colleges get even halfway there—to the level of "minimum professional proficiency." In 1965, 90 per cent of the graduating French majors failed to reach the level of minimum professional proficiency in speaking, and only half of them reached that level in reading (Carroll 1967, 14, 89). The so-called "reading knowledge" of a language required for a Ph.D. degree is an even lower level of proficiency, equivalent to just passing a second-year college language course (Harvey 1968). Very few American scholars can do serious research in languages other than English. Even linguists have all too tellingly proclaimed that they are not polyglots. Roman Jakobson likes to tell how Professor Antoine Meillet of Paris and Professor Edgar Sturtevant of Yale, two of the world's great Indo-European linguists of the last generation, had to talk to each other through an interpreter when they met.

But in spite of the widespread failure at language learning, we all know of people who had spectacular success at becoming bilingual. One's own grandfather, perhaps, was

1

born in Europe—in a bilingual area of Switzerland, say, where he went to school five days a week in French and the sixth day in German. At age fourteen this grandfather might have come to America to spend a year in a one-room schoolhouse getting an eighth grade education in English. The result was a person who had soon mastered English and who had native speaker proficiency (at the eighth grade level) in three languages.

The discrepancy between the successes and the failures in foreign language learning is so embarrassing to teachers that it has made language acquisition the most emotion-ridden and controversial aspect of linguistic theory. And the "new" methods for language teaching which are continually being invented are advertised as if they were patent medicines for some heretofore incurable ailment.

The major language acquisition controversy has been that of the "empiricists" vs. the "rationalists," to use Chomsky's terms (Chomsky 1965, 47-48). Both of these theoretical traditions have long histories and several different methods of language teaching which try to carry out their theoretical presuppositions about what language is and how it is learned.

If we ignore this long-standing theoretical division between rationalists and empiricists, the history of foreign language teaching is terribly confusing and doesn't make sense. Books on language teaching usually have a chapter on history which names off a selection of different teaching methods that have followed one another down through the centuries. There was the Ollendorf method, the Jacotot method, the natural method, the imitative method, the series method, the direct method, the reading method, the Army method, the grammar method, the translation method, the inductive method, the linguistic method, the oral method, the aural-oral method, the audio-lingual method, maybe a dozen or so other methods, and now, finally the author's "new" method.

These histories are not very satisfactory, because they usually fail to show any relationship between the various methods. All methods seem to have emerged full-blown from their creators' heads, with no debt to previous teachers and no effect on later ones. These histories seem to imply that there were no theoretical justifications for the older methods, and that the old-fashioned methods were all created un-thinkingly for *ad hoc* situations. The net effect is not of history at all, but of a catalog of unrelated and apparently unsuccessful teaching methods.

Descriptive linguists have sometimes tried to impose order on the chaos of methods. They have even brought in some theoretical considerations—but only to assert that until American descriptive linguists got into the act in World War II, there were no scientifically based language teaching methods. Robert Lado, for example, in his *Language Teaching: A Scientific Approach* (1964), says that first there was the classical grammar-translation method. But this hardly qualifies as language teaching, since people weren't taught to speak. Then everyone who taught a spoken language before World War II is said to have used the "direct method." He mentions Viëtor, Jespersen, and Palmer as proponents of this direct method. Then, he says, "the advocates of the direct method, failing to achieve decisive results for a variety of reasons, drifted in the 1930's into a more limited goal of a reading knowledge. This was a purely passive understanding of graded readings with dictionary help on difficult words" (Lado 1964, 5). Finally, then, linguists came along with a scientific approach, and created methods of mimicry, memorization, and pattern drill for the Army Specialized Training Program in World War II.

Lado has a nice simple schema for the history of language teaching. The only trouble is that it is simply wrong. First of all, Jespersen and Palmer were not proponents of the "direct method." Jespersen explicitly dissociated himself from Gouin and Berlitz (both of whom did propose direct methods), and he rejected the term "direct method" as quite inappropriate for what he called his "imitative method" of language teaching (Jespersen 1904, 2). Palmer stated that "the exclusion of the mother tongue is generally, if not always, a vicious procedure productive of the most harmful results" (Palmer 1917, 251). That statement alone is enough to disqualify Palmer's method as a "direct method." In reality, Jespersen and Palmer and a whole host of late nine-teenth-century linguists (Jespersen lists Sweet, Storm, Sievers, Sayce, and Lundell) were direct precursors to the mimicry, memorization, and pattern drill of twentieth-century American linguists. As Einar Haugen has pointed out, every one of Leonard Bloomfield's ideas on language teaching "builds on the references he gives to European writers, and particularly Otto Jespersen" (Haugen 1955, 244). Mimicry and memorization play a central role in Jespersen's methodology, and he calls for a version of pattern drill as well. Palmer also was in favor of mimicry and memorization, and in 1916 he came out with the first published book of pattern drills for English as a foreign language. In short, ever since the 1880's linguists have had their methods of mimicry, memorization, and pattern drill, and ever since that time there has been a controversy between these linguists and others (like Gouin, Berlitz, and de Sauzé) who argued for direct methods.

There is also no basis for Lado's assertion that proponents of the direct method failed to achieve decisive results and went over to the reading method. It is true that Algernon Coleman recommended the reading method in a report issued under the auspices of the Modern Foreign Language Study (Coleman 1929). But no advocate of the direct method accepted Coleman's report. A dissenting statement was issued by three members of the committee of direction and control of the Modern Foreign Language Study, and Coleman took upon himself sole responsibility for his report, absolving other participants in the study from its recommendations. An open letter attacking the Coleman report was signed by eighty-six leading advocates of the direct method, and was published in the *Modern Language Journal* (Mercier et al. 1931).[1] The direct method did not die out at all, but is alive and flourishing—particularly in the Berlitz schools (where it has been going strong for more than 90 years), and in the Cleveland public schools where they have been using Emile B. de Sauzé 's Cleveland Plan for more than 50 years. Recently a number of new textbooks have appeared which are outgrowths of de Sauzé 's experience. [2]

----

[1] On the politics of the Modern Foreign Language Study, see also Barall 1949, Morgan 1930, Meras 1931, and Mercier 1931.
[2] Lénard 1965, 1969, Pucciani and Hamel 1967, Traversa 1967, Pfister 1968.

Why did Lado and the other descriptive linguists overlook the fact that ever since the 1880's there has been a controversy between proponents of the direct methods and the linguists who favored mimicry, memorization, and pattern drills? There are at least two reasons. First, they were so sure about the correctness of their scientific linguistics that they could not even conceive that other theories of grammar had enough validity to cause legitimate controversy. They had a *new* approach to language which they thought superseded all other theories of grammar without serious argument. Second, the emphasis on new scientific developments blinded them to the fact that Leonard Bloomfield had European predecessors. Thus Mary R. Haas could write in 1943 that "Principles first used in recording American Indian languages have been applied to the teaching of Oriental languages with unexpectedly good results" (Haas 1943, 203), completely ignoring the fact, as Haugen pointed out (1955), that these principles had been used by European linguists to describe non-Indian languages and that indeed the principles had already been applied to the teaching of European languages. But newness has always been highly valued by the descriptive linguists, and in 1960 Charles C. Fries was still maintaining that his was "A New Approach to Language Learning"; in 1965 Belasco and Valdman brought out their *College French in the New Key*; and in 1966 Robert A. Hall, Jr. published a book on *New Ways to Learn a Foreign Language*—all advocating a method that was already highly developed in 1916.

It should seem obvious that the history of foreign language teaching did not have a linear development. We do not have a situation in which the faults of one method were corrected by a new method, each one superseding the last. Rather, we have two separate histories. The great theoretical division between linguists—the empiricists vs. the rationalists—also divides the language teaching methodologies. Teachers on the one side include Jespersen, Palmer, and the other European linguists of the "reform method," along with Leonard Bloomfield and his following of American descriptive linguists—all having an "empiricist" or "behaviorist" theory of language acquisition. On the other side we have François

Gouin, M. D. Berlitz, Emile de Sauzé, and many other traditional grammarians with a "rationalist" theory of language acquisition very similar to that of Chomsky's transformational generative grammar.

In the empiricist camp, the teaching methods have been for the most part variations on the imitative methods of mimicry and memorization with pattern drills. Sometimes you get "mim-mem" alone, as in Y. R. Chao's *Mandarin Primer* (1961); and sometimes you have almost nothing but pattern drills, as in Lado and Fries's *Intensive Course in English* (1958). But the most sophisticated, from Palmer to *Modern Spanish* (Bolinger et al. 1960), have always combined the two.

Mim-mem and pattern drill as methods follow directly from the basic empiricist position that language acquisition is a kind of habit formation through conditioning and drill. Descriptive linguists have affirmed that the normal use of language is either mimicry or analogy; grammatical rules are merely descriptions of habits, and in normal fast speech, they say, a person has no time to apply rules as recipes for sentence formation. In its behaviorist extreme, as held by many descriptive linguists, the empiricist position maintains that human beings use basically the same learning processes as other animals do—a stimulus-response model of conditioning. Leonard Bloomfield, an avowed behaviorist, maintained that vocal human language is not essentially different from gesture language or animal language (Bloomfield 1914, 14). Some people in the empiricist tradition have maintained that the mind is a "blank tablet" upon which the outside world imposes various sorts of knowledge; the behaviorists refuse to go so far as to talk of "knowledge" or of "mind"—for them the human being is essentially a machine with a collection of habits which have been molded by the outside world.

In the rationalist camp there has been more variety in teaching methods, ranging from the ill-conceived grammar-translation method, through Gouin's highly original "series method" to the tightly organized "direct methods" of Berlitz and de Sauzé. From the very first day, the direct methods have the students generate original and meaningful sentences in order for them to gain a functional knowledge of the rules of grammar. This emphasis follows directly from the rationalist position that man is born with the ability to think and to learn a specialized cognitive code called human language. Man is equipped with a highly organized brain that permits certain kinds of mental activity which are impossible for other animals—among other things, he is the only animal that can learn human languages (and virtually all human beings learn at least one language). The rationalist notes that on an abstract level, all languages work in the same way—they all have words and sentences and sound systems and grammatical relations—and he attributes these universals of language to the structure of the brain. Just as birds inherit the ability to fly, and fish to swim, men inherit the ability to think and to use language in a manner which is unique to their species. A given language, English, for example, has to be learned, but the capacity to learn languages is inherited. The child is not a passive agent in language acquisition; he actively goes about learning the language of his environment. Language use becomes almost automatic, but what a person learns is more than a set of conditioned habits. If you read all the books in the English language, you will find very few sentences which are habitually used and are exact duplicates of each other —otherwise you would suspect quotation or plagiarism. Knowledge of a language allows a person to understand infinitely many new sentences, and to create grammatical sentences which no one else has ever pronounced but which will be understood immediately by others who know the language.

Descriptive linguists, the "establishment" until very recently, have generally tried to denigrate or ignore the direct-method teachers and their rationalist presuppositions. They make snide remarks about Berlitz ("The 'conversation -method' reminds us perhaps too much of Berlitz schools," says Jesperson (1904, 2)). The highly successful materials of de Sauzé are not mentioned in the modest bibliographies of Politzer (1960) or Brooks (1964) or even in the Modern Language Association's 1962 *Selective List of Materials.* The gulf between empiricist and rationalist is so wide that there is hardly any communication between them.

Viewed, then, from the standpoint of theory, the history of foreign language teaching begins to take intelligible shape. We have two major traditions of language teaching, based on two different views of language and language acquisition. Decisions on language teaching methodology have not been primarily the result of practical and disinterested experimentation; they have been decisions based instead on differing theories of language. It has become commonplace, especially since N. R. Hanson's discussion of the *Patterns of Discovery* (1958), that a scientist's theoretical prejudices will control to a large measure the facts which he will choose to see and those he will fail to notice. It is not surprising, then, that linguists have been blind to facts which do not fit their theories, and that they have been adept at finding facts which seem to support their theories of language acquisition. Language teaching methods are manifestations of linguistic presuppositions, and for the most part are variations on two themes—the empiricist and rationalist theories of language learning.

Two very different theories of how languages are learned, then, have fostered two very different conceptions of how foreign languages ought to be taught. The history of language teaching methodology, like the history of linguistic theory, is a dual history—each stream having its own separate development.

PART II

THEORIES
OF
LANGUAGE
LEARNING

CHAPTER 2

THE EMPIRICIST APPROACH OF
STRUCTURAL LINGUISTICS

In the forties and fifties, American structural linguists brought about a reform of language teaching in the United States. Like many other successful reformers, they reduced their main principles to a set of slogans to be followed. William Moulton (1961), in his review of those decades of reform, put down this formulation of the slogans:

1) "Language is speech, not writing."
2) "A language is a set of habits."
3) "Teach the language, not about the language."
4) "A language is what its native speakers say, not what someone thinks they ought to say."
5) "Languages are different."[3]

Notice that nothing is said here about "methods" of teaching; we have only the theoretical approach to language teaching.

---

[3] Similar sets of principles have been articulated by a large number of linguist-language teachers, including Jespersen 1904 (with certain reservations); Palmer 1917 and 1921; Bloomfield 1942; Haas 1943 and 1953; O'Connor and Twaddell 1960; Anthony 1963; Bolinger et al. 1963; Lado 1964; Rivers 1964; Brooks 1964; and H. B. Allen 1965b.

Moulton regards these slogans as good formulations of the "linguistic principles" on which the structural linguists based their language teaching. On the surface it may seem that some of the slogans are gratuitous—"teach the language, not about the language"—in what sense is this a controversial statement from a theoretical point of view? The controversy comes in the definition of terms, particularly in what is meant by "language." Here, as defined by slogan number two, "a language is a set of habits." If we take these slogans with the meaning that was originally intended, embodying the whole structuralist or descriptivist view of language, then no one in the rationalist tradition can agree with them. So let us turn our attention to what is behind each of these slogans and point out why a rationalist would disagree with them.

1. *Language is speech, not writing*

At first, it appears that the intent of this slogan is to play down the role of the written language in language teaching. All normal children, of course, learn to speak before they learn to write. And on a little reflection it becomes evident that a majority of the human beings who have lived in this world have been illiterate; yet virtually all of them knew a spoken language.

But the hang-up of the structural linguists is not the writing systems which they might want to avoid; it is the spoken aspect of language which concerns them—speech, phonology, pronunciation. I say "spoken aspect of language," because it is not at all obvious that "language *is* speech." In fact, this proposition is falsified by the single case history described by Lenneberg (1967, 305) of a boy who was physically unable to articulate a single speech sound. Yet this boy learned English, and understood it fully (he could take orders from a tape recorder) and he learned to read.

It would seem, from this boy's case, that the rationalists are correct in maintaining that language is primarily a cognitive matter. But the descriptive linguists have refused to admit that "knowledge" of a language might be primarily a matter of the mind, of mental activity. The "descriptivists" will describe only what they can observe. They are after concrete facts. The "mind" cannot be observed; therefore, it must not exist. As Twaddell (1935, 57n) put it, "The scientific method is quite simply the convention that mind does not exist." And the descriptive linguists want above all things to make their study of language a truly "scientific" study.

By definition, then, language becomes a collection of concrete observable signs. Saussure and others would allow abstract signs, but these always had to be derivable from concrete tangible signs (Saussure 1915, 190-191). Joos expressed this principle as a "neo-Saussurean axiom" that "Text signals its own structure" (Joos 1961, 17). There is no hidden structure which cannot be observed directly.

"Descriptivism" leads in this way directly to "structuralism." The concrete signs of language have a "structure" rather than a rule-governed grammar, and the structure is made from various building blocks. The fundamental units of structural descriptions are the distinctive sounds of language, the *phonemes*. These sounds are combined into meaningful units, *morphemes*. Then we make words out of morphemes (*blackberries* has three morphemes: *black, berry,* and *s*). Finally we make phrases and sentences out of words.

No "understood" but absent elements are allowed in the description of a sentence. Traditional grammarians would say that imperative sentences (e.g., "Come!") have the subject "*you* understood." But Bloomfield and other structuralists held it to be meaningless to talk of an "understood" subject when no subject is expressed (Bloomfield 1933, 170).

Saussure maintains, in like manner, that "In English *the man I have seen* apparently uses a zero sign to stand for a syntactical fact which French expresses by *que* 'that' (l'homme *que* j'ai vu). But," he says, "the comparing of the English with the French syntactical fact is precisely what produces the illusion that nothingness can create something" (Saussure 1915, 139). Saussure does not notice that English is quite able to express the "que" by the fuller form in "the man *that* I have seen." Indeed, without expressing the "that," the English phrase is ambiguous and can be used in two very different senses, as in "The man I have seen had red hair" and "The man I have seen, but not the woman." There is a double dilemma for the structuralist in this example: first, in truly ambiguous utterances the text does not signal its own structure unambiguously—but perhaps that can be explained away as a defect in language and not in structuralism; second, does the presence of "that" have any structural significance in "the man that I have seen"? If so, why isn't the structure changed when "that" is deleted from the phrase? Structuralism can't really explain this second dilemma away.

As a result of these dilemmas of syntax, structural linguists tried to ignore sentence formation as much as possible. Saussure, for example, relegated sentence formation to individual acts of speaking (*parole*); it was not a part of the language (*langue*) (Saussure 1915, 124). Sentences were generally thought to be built up by analogy to the structural patterns of sentences previously heard. Bloomfield would say then, that "the utterance last spoken will alter the conditions of the next one . . . the language even of a single individual is never exactly the same in any two utterances. What unity there is is due to the assimilative effect of earlier upon later actions" (Bloomfield 1914, 259). And as Hockett phrased it, "whenever a person speaks, he is either mimicking or analogizing" (Hockett 1958, 425).

In this fluid situation, the sounds of the language provide the only solid base, and phonological analysis is the first task of the linguist. Thus behind the slogan "Language is speech, not writing," we find structuralism's obsession with phonology, which expresses itself in a desire to have the language student master the pronunciation of a foreign language above all else.

2. A language is a set of habits

In trying to do away with "knowledge" and "mind," descriptive linguists assumed that a language was a set of (speech) habits, acquired by conditioning. This is "habit" in a very narrow sense. Bloomfield described the child's acquisition of language in five steps: 1) First, the baby begins to babble—apparently because of an inherited trait. He eventually gains the habit of repeating a given mouth movement when he hears its corresponding sound. That is, he gains the ability to say *da-da-da* instead of just *da*. 2) Then when someone says *doll* in the baby's presence, the child hears *da* and repeats *da*. The child has begun to imitate. 3) The mother says *doll* so often in front of the baby's doll, that, in Bloomfield's words, "the child forms a new habit: the sight and feel of the doll suffice to make him say *da*." This is *classical conditioning*. 4) The habit of saying *da* when he sees his doll can be turned into abstract or displaced speech by a further process of classical conditioning. Suppose, Bloomfield suggests, that the child then gains the habit of saying *da* after his bath. But one day the mother forgets to give the baby the doll. When he says *da* this time, the mother interprets it as a question: the baby is asking for his doll. Thus the child begins to ask for things not present. 5) The child's speech is "perfected by its results" (*operant conditioning*). The closer the baby's *da* is to the parents' *doll*, the more likely it will be that the parents bring the doll when it is asked for. Bad pronunciation will be extinguished by lack of the desired results (Bloomfield 1933, 19-31).

This is Bloomfield's model for how a child could learn to speak without thinking. The nice thing about this model is that it is so simple. William Dwight Whitney, who held a similar position (1872; 1875) was not at all surprised at the child's ability to learn languages. As he says, "a child, after hearing a certain word used some scores or hundreds of times, comes to understand what it means, and then, a little later, to pronounce and use it, perhaps feebly and blundering-ly at first—this does not seem to us any more astonishing than the exercise of the same child's capacities in other directions; in acquiring, for instance, the command of a musical instrument" (Whitney 1872, 269).

Perhaps the most serious recent attempt to work out the mechanism of language as a set of habits is that of B.F. Skinner (1957).[4] Skinner is an extreme behaviorist, and his

[4] Unfortunately, the task was so difficult and complex that, as Chomsky points out (1959), even the most fundamental terms of behaviorism—"stimulus," "response," "reinforcement"—could not be taken literally. These terms had to be extended metaphorically from their literal meaning as defined in experimentation, and therefore Skinner's attempt at a behaviorist explanation of language failed.

definition of verbal behavior even "includes the behavior of experimental animals where reinforcements are supplied by an experimenter or by an apparatus designed to establish contingencies which resemble those maintained by the normal listener. The animal and the experimenter comprise a small but genuine verbal community" (Skinner 1957, 108n). Yet Bloomfield stated virtually the same position in 1914 when he maintained that vocal human language is not essentially different from gesture language or animal language (Bloomfield 1914, 14). Recent discussions by linguists of foreign language learning have also been close to the Skinnerian view. Wilga Rivers (1964) has amassed a number of quotations to show that many descriptive linguists are very close to the extreme Skinnerian view.

If this view of language learning seems a bit facile, it is not inconsistent with the structuralist view that "text signals its own structure." This theory does not require the child to learn an abstract system of rules relating the speech signal to an abstract underlying structure. "Whenever a person speaks he is either mimicking or analogizing." All one needs to do is mimic a few basic sentences, and then make new ones by analogy as the occasion arises. This is the basis for the methods of "mim-mem and pattern drill." Memorization speeds up the process of establishing the basic treasury of sentences which can be extended by analogy; pattern drill provides the practice in making the analogies.

3. Teach the language, not about the language

All too often after many hours of traditional language study, a student has been able to recite paradigms and grammar rules, but has been totally unable to speak the language which he has studied. Our third slogan arose in reaction to that situation. As Moulton says, "The real goal of instruction was an ability to *talk* the language, and not to talk *about* it" (1961, 88). This was a goal which people in both the "empiricist" and "rationalist" camps could accept. Gouin, Berlitz, and de Sauzé, for example, were emphatically in favor of teaching people to talk the language. Nevertheless, when the empiricist linguist said "Teach the language, not about the language," he intended something which no rationalist linguist could accept.

In reading this slogan it is important to remember that a "language" is considered to be a "set of habits"; we are thus being asked to teach a set of habits, not a set of rules for sentence formation. This is another reflection of the "descriptiveness" of descriptive linguistics. It is maintained that the "grammatical rule" has no psychological reality. The rule is a description of a habit, and nothing more. There is no possibility that the linguist's rule of grammar might be a description of some sort of mental rule by which (perhaps without conscious thought) a speaker forms sentences; instead, the rule of grammar is a summary of behavior. As Twaddell put it, "We know that a 'rule' of a language is the analytical statement of one of the habitual aspects of that language. We know that the habit is the reality and the rule is a mere summary of the habit" (1948, 77-78). The context for this statement by Twaddell is a paper on "Meanings, Habits, and Rules," in which he argues that we think about *what* we say, not *how* we say it (a statement made many times by other linguists). Therefore, *what* we say involves "meanings"; *how* we say it does not. Twaddell remarks on the fact that students invariably want to regard "grammatical habits as meanings." They want to pay close attention to matters which should be wholly automatic. This is an entirely mistaken attitude on the part of the student, Twaddell argues, and it is the teacher's duty to keep the student from consciously thinking about *how* to speak. A grammatical description can be presented for purposes of a liberal education, or even perhaps as an aid to memory, but this description may come only after the habit has been formed by the student.[5]

[5] It should not be inferred that the linguists' emphasis on not teaching about the language led to textbooks which contained little structural description. Quite the contrary was the case. The descriptive notes in textbooks by linguists were often very extensive, and in many cases—those of the "exotic languages" in particular—this material was quite original and valuable to linguistics. Sometimes the linguist authors of textbooks expected the structural notes to be read at home and ignored in class. But in the Army Specialized Training Program, when linguist-informant teams were used to teach languages, the plans called for frequent lectures on linguistic structure given in the native language of the students. In the Cornell adaptation of the Army program, as much as one fourth of the class time was devoted to lectures in English by linguists (cf. Moulton 1952).

Note the distinction in terminology between a "structural description" of habits and a "grammar" for generating sentences. As one recent statement put it, "The word *structure* is used here in preference to the word *grammar.* . . . The word structure denotes an emphasis slightly different from the grammar concept in that the students master the structure of the language as a conditioned response, while the grammarians are more inclined to lead the students to reason out their answers according to the 'rules' " (Mueller and Leutenegger 1964, 91).

So in our slogan, to "teach the language" is to impose a set of conditioned speech habits on a student who, as far as we can observe, is not in possession of a mind and is incapable of mental activity. Building up speech habits in this way requires essentially rote methods, and mim-mem and pattern drill are well suited to this goal. Not to teach "about the language" is to avoid giving grammatical rules for sentence formation, since the notion of rule following is inconceivable in the behaviorist tradition.

4. A language is what its native speakers say, not what someone thinks they ought to say

This slogan furthers the attack on rules and goes against the whole concept of grammaticality.

Prescriptive school grammars were the first to be attacked, of course. After all, few educated Americans really adhere to the artificial uses of *shall* and *will,* of *who* and *whom,* which these grammars tried to teach.

Bloomfield and other linguists would not tolerate the suggestion that the formal dialect taught in schools was "more correct" than dialects learned on the farm or in the slums. Bloomfield agreed that the speech of some people was more prestigious than that of others. But the imitation of these prestigious dialects as if they were more correct is "snobbery" (Bloomfield 1933, chapter 28). This attitude was echoed by other linguists—notably by Robert Hall in his books *Leave Your Language Alone!* (1950) and *Hands Off Pidgin English!* (1955). A number of polemical articles with this point of view are reprinted in H. B. Allen (1958).

But the attack on prescriptive grammar went much farther—so far as to leave no doctrine of grammaticality at all. There were no standards even within a single individual. A native speaker could not make a mistake. As Moulton says, in foreign-language teaching the linguist-teacher would tell his students "to 'copy what the native speaker says,' whether or not it agreed with what was in the textbook, because 'the native speaker is always right'" (Moulton 1961, 89). Such distinctions as Chomsky's "competence" vs. "performance" are not acceptable in this view. It is not conceivable that a speaker could know how to say something and then say it wrong. Discussion of what a speaker "knows" is taboo in this "scientific descriptive linguistics," so everything which a speaker does has to be correct. In English, for example, adverbs of place precede adverbs of time: "I will go *there tomorrow.*" If by mistake a person said, "I will go tomorrow there," the descriptive linguist would not want to admit that the speaker (if he were a native) had uttered an un-grammatical sentence. At best the user of that sentence would be described as having an unusual dialect. But surely this native speaker couldn't have made a mistake.

A. A. Hill has taken that position, for example, in an article on "Grammaticality" (1961). He argues that any spoken utterance is given a normal intonation pattern and that therefore no spoken utterance can be ungrammatical. If someone says, "I saw a fragile of" (cf. Chomsky 1957, 16), Hill would have us respond with "What's an *of*?". We should not consider that this might be an ungrammatical sentence ending with a familiar preposition. Hill refers to a sentence which Henry Lee Smith, Jr., had called ungrammatical: "Tall the man cigar the smoked black." But Hill explains away even this sentence: "Smith, a leading if not the leading exponent of phonologically based grammar and syntax, seems here to have been hasty, impelled by the necessity of giving an ungrammatical example in a popular article where he could not indicate the intonation. One wonders whether his meaning is not approximately 'This is a sequence of words for which it would be difficult to find a suitable intonation pattern.' One can be found, however. *Man cigar* can be read with the stress of a nominal compound, and the utterance as a whole read as two linked equations. The fact that the meaning remains unknown is irrelevant" (Hill 1961, 8n).

But if deviations are acceptable in the speech of natives, the same tolerance is not extended to foreigners. Foreigners *can* make mistakes. Teachers in the empiricist approach have had a profound fear of mistakes, because mistakes are seen as the first step in forming bad habits. Memorization of authentic sentences spoken by native speakers is therefore extremely important. The more memorization the better, for then the student will have a large stock of genuine sentences on which to base his analogies. By the same token, pattern drills should be designed so that students will almost never make mistakes. If to learn a language is to copy what the native speaker says, rote methods are in order.

5. *Languages are different*

Leonard Bloomfield began his *Outline Guide for the Practical Study of Foreign Languages* by stressing the point that the language learner must "start with a clean slate" because "the sounds, constructions, and meanings of different languages are not the same." Bloomfield tells us to forget what we learned in school or college ("what little they teach is largely in error"), and above all, the student "must learn to ignore the features of any and all other languages, especially of one's own" (Bloomfield 1942, 1).

Everyone recognizes that foreign accents are mistakes in pronunciation which are caused by interference from the foreigner's native language. It has been thought that the chief obstacle to foreign language learning by adults is the interference between his old and new sets of habits. So the descriptive linguist reasons that a) the student should ignore his old language habits, and b) language-learning materials should give special emphasis to drilling the matters most likely to conflict. The teacher, then, should follow the exact opposite of what Bloomfield advised for the student; instead of ignoring the features of all languages known by the student, he should pay very close attention to these features and try to predict where the most serious interference between habit systems will develop. Thus contrastive studies were made between languages, and a new discipline arose —contrastive linguistics.

Many linguists held that contrastive structural analysis was the single most important contribution which they could make to foreign-language teaching. This was Fries's view, for example, and Lado's (Fries 1945; Lado 1957). From this point of view, the structure of the student's native language was at least as important to the textbook writer as was the structure of the language to be taught. Fries and his associates at the English Language Institute of the University of Michigan worked out materials in English as a foreign language for Latin American students (Lado and Fries 1958 is a revision of materials written in the early 1940's). Then they started over again for speakers of Chinese (Fries and Shen, 1946). Apparently, however, they did not think it worthwhile to develop special sets of curriculum for speakers of other languages. And the course for Latin American students was revised in 1958 to be used by foreigners of all backgrounds.

In recent years the number of published contrastive studies has been increasing very fast. The Center for Applied Linguistics has issued two bibliographies on contrastive studies between English and other languages. The bibliography of 1961 had about 200 items listed; in 1965 there were almost 500 (Gage 1961; Hammer 1965; cf. Ferguson 1966, 55).

Everyone, of course, holds some version of the doctrine that "languages are different"; difference is implied when we talk of languages in the plural. For the descriptive linguists, however, it means (in theory, at least) that there are no linguistic universals. As Joos expressed it, "languages could differ from each other unpredictably and without limit" (Joos 1958, 96).[6]

Charles Ferguson has pointed out that, as he says, "contrastive analysis presents the descriptivist with his basic

---

[6] Joos attributed this view to Boas; Teeter more correctly calls this the "post-Boasian fallacy" of American linguistics. Teeter points out that combined with the "post-Bloomfieldian fallacy" which dropped the assumption of the mind, linguistics was left with little else but field methods, and linguistic theory became equated with the methodology for describing languages (Teeter 1964).

dilemma in its sharpest form" (Ferguson 1963, 121). On the one hand, the descriptivist wants to describe each language on its own terms, and not in terms of universal categories. Yet in order to compare such things as "noun systems" or "phonemic systems," he is forced to use the universal categories "noun" and "phoneme." In other words, when Bloomfield says "The sounds, constructions, and meanings of different languages are not the same . . .", he is implying that all languages *do* have sounds, constructions, and meanings, even if the second half of his sentence states that ". . . to get an easy command of a foreign language one must learn to ignore the features of any and all other languages, especially of one's own" (Bloomfield 1942, 1).

When Bloomfield warned students to shed their prepossessions about language and to start with a clean slate, he was trying to warn them not to be misled by supposed universals of language. The one fact about language which the linguist wanted his student to learn was that since languages were different, he should expect everything in the new language to be different from his native language. For example, Waldo Sweet includes a little introduction to linguistics at the beginning of his textbook *Latin: A Structural Approach* (1957). There are four chapters, all stressing that languages are different: sound systems differ, languages "fit together" differently, vocabulary structure is different, and English is different from a supposed universal grammar.

If someone suggests that an American who knows Spanish already will be able to learn French more quickly, it will be countered that related languages are especially misleading and that this person's French will show mistakes caused by two languages instead of just by one.[7]

For the empiricists, then, students should merely memorize the genuine utterances of native speakers and allow the habits of the language to be imposed upon them.

---

[7] There was a bitter polemic exchange between Bolling and Whatmough on this point. To Whatmough it was obvious that it was to a student's advantage to have already studied other languages. He was utterly scornful of Bloomfield's exhortation to "start with a clean slate" (see Whatmough 1944 and references cited there).

CHAPTER 3

THE RATIONALIST APPROACH TO
LANGUAGE LEARNING

Since the late 1950's an increasingly large number of linguists have followed Noam Chomsky and other generative grammarians in rejecting the empiricist approach to language learning in favor of a sophisticated revival of the rationalist approach. Generative grammarians themselves have not yet established themselves in the language teaching profession to the extent that the structuralists have, but rationalist-based "direct methods" similar to those of Berlitz and de Sauzé are undergoing a spirited revival in this new linguistic climate.

Let us organize our discussion of the rationalist approach around four propositions: 1) A living language is characterized by rule-governed creativity. 2) The rules of grammar are psychologically real. 3) Man is uniquely built to learn languages. 4) A living language is a language in which we can think.

1. A living language is characterized by rule-governed creativity

"An intelligent adult is rarely successful in mastering a foreign language," says de Sauzé, "without learning in a functional way certain fundamental principles that govern the structure of that language and that enable him to generalize, to multiply his experience a thousand times. To know by memory even an ample stock of ready-made sentences in a language is not the same as to know that language" (de Sauzé 1929, 4). Except for purposes of quotation, people rarely have occasion to use sentences that they have heard other people use. If people used the sentences of this book without acknowledging the quotation, they would be guilty of plagiarism. To know a language is to be able to create *new* sentences in the language. In Chomsky's words, "normal linguistic behavior . . . is stimulus free and innovative" (Chomsky 1966b, 46). In most situations it is quite impossible to predict what will be said. The "stimulus" of this book, for example, will bring out different "responses" from every reader. Such stimuli obviously do not determine the responses.

But if language use is basically innovative, it is innovative only within the bounds of grammaticality. Not all collections of English words result in grammatical sentences. In fact, the chances are not great that you could find any six consecutive head words in a dictionary that would produce a grammatical sentence: somnolent son sonance sonant sonar sonata.

It is the grammar that allows us to tell the difference between *The man led the horse too fast* and *The fast horse led the man, too*. In a grammatical sentence we know what the subjects and predicates are. In the first sentence above, we know that the man did the leading and that "too" modifies "fast," making an adverbial phrase which tells us more about this particular act of leading. In the second sentence, the horse himself is fast and does the leading, and "too" modifies the whole sentence.

Take the sentence quoted by Hill, above, "Tall the man cigar the smoked black." This sentence is clearly not grammatical. What is the subject? the predicate? What is the grammatical function of "black"? It is *not* irrelevant that the meaning remains unknown. In spite of the English words, this is not an English sentence.

The limitations of grammaticality rule out a large number of word combinations, but in spite of this the innovative power of language is theoretically infinite. There can be no limit to the length of sentences, and thus no limit to the number of different grammatical sentences. A given sentence can always be lengthened by absorbing other sentences into it. Many long parliamentary resolutions, with all their long "whereas" clauses, are no more than one sentence long—and we can always add another "whereas . . .". But suppose we arbitrarily set a limit of 20 words for grammatical sentences. How many would we have then? George Miller has made a conservative estimate that there are at least 10^{20} grammatical twenty-word sentences in English. "Putting it differently," he says, "it would take 100,000,000,000 centuries (one thousand times the estimated age of the earth) to utter all the admissible twenty-word sentences of English. Thus the probability that you might have heard any particular twenty-word sentence before is negligible. Unless it is a cliché, every sentence must come to you as a novel combination of morphemes. Yet you can interpret it at once if you know the English language" (Miller 1964b, 299).[8]

This is to say that an infinite number of sentences can be produced by what seems to be a rather small finite number of grammatical rules. A speaker does not have to store a large number of ready-made sentences in his head; he just needs the rules for creating and understanding these sentences.

In foreign-language learning, understanding the fundamental rules of grammar can "multiply [our] experience a thousand times." That is to say that a conscious effort at figuring out how to say things will be rather more efficient than hoping that we will unconsciously learn how to say things if we memorize enough basic sentences. As de Sauzé puts it, "We found, also, in our experiment that the practical results, such as reading, writing, speaking, and understanding, were achieved in greater proportion and in less time when the technique involved a maximum amount of conscious reasoning" de Sauzé 1959, 5).

---

[8] This estimate does not include the infinite set of sentences containing numbers ("It is at least one second since I began talking." "It is at least two seconds since I began talking."...).

2. The rules of grammar are psychologically real

Linguists are sometimes hesitant to say that ordinary
people "know" the rules of their language, because linguists
themselves have such a hard time trying to formulate these
rules explicitly. Leonard Bloomfield, for example, seemed to
doubt whether unschooled people could isolate the different
words of a sentence (Bloomfield 1942, 13). But words are
obviously psychologically real units. When children learn to
speak, the first thing they do is to isolate words. Only later
do they combine them into sentences, and it is even later
before they add the grammatical inflections and the articles
(*a, an, the*). A second piece of evidence is pig Latin, a secret
language that requires the speaker to know not only about
words but about initial consonant clusters. Not only do
children learn pig Latin easily, they have no trouble
"learning" that the sounds of a language are discrete elements
which can be represented by the letters of the alphabet.
Besides knowing about words and about discrete sounds,
children also know that the sounds are made up of *distinctive
features*. They may not be able to formulate this knowledge
for you, but they know that the final sounds of *judge,
church, bush, bus,* and *fez* form a natural class of strident
consonants. Children know that the plural ending after
strident consonants is pronounced [iz] (as in *buses*), and that
after other sounds it is pronounced either [z] or [s]
depending on whether those sounds are voiced or not (as in
cars, trucks). Experiments have shown that this is a productive rule which children apply to nonsense words (Berko
1958). (If this is a *zug*, what are those?—They're *zugs*
[pronounced zugz], too.)[9]

But if children are not able to formulate the rules of
grammar which they use, in what sense can we say that they
"know" these rules? This is the question that has bothered
linguists. The answer is that *they know the rules in a
functional way*, in a way which relates the changes in abstract

[9] On the psychological reality of abstract phonological elements, see
also Halle 1962, 1964, Sapir 1933, O'Neil 1966, Chomsky and
Halle 1968.

grammatical structure to changes in meaning. Knowledge does not always have to be formulated. Children can use tools before they learn the names for these tools.

The key distinction to note here is *the difference between a rule and a formulation of a rule.* For example, Max Black has pointed out that there is a rule of chess to the effect that "A pawn on reaching the eighth rank must be exchanged for a piece." But there are other equally good formulations of the rule, among which Black lists these: "Pawns shall be promoted on reaching the end of the chessboard"; "Pawns reaching the last rank are replaced by pieces"; and "Pawns must be replaced by pieces whenever a further move would carry them off the chessboard." Further, as Black points out, "each of these formulations could be translated into German, or any other language containing names for chess pieces and their moves . . . . It follows from this that it would be a mistake to identify the rule about the promotion of pawns with any one of its formulations. For there is the one rule, but indefinitely many formulations of it" (Black 1962, 101). Knowing a rule and being able to act on it is quite independent of being able to formulate the rule adequately. The rule can be psychologically real without any formulation of it.

It is worthwhile pursuing the matter of rule following in chess, as it can help clear up some of the problems regarding rule following in language. It is essential that chess be played according to the rules. If a player tries to move a rook diagonally across the chessboard (in *analogy* to the way bishops move), he is making an illegal move, and his opponent will surely stop him from this action. Legality in chess moves is like grammaticality in language. Just as we say "you can't do that in chess," we object to ungrammatical sentences with "you can't say it that way in English."

The chief argument given by the empiricists that language is a set of habits, not rules, is that language use is automatic and not on a level of intellectual awareness. As O'Connor and Twaddell put it, "There is no time for puzzle-solving or applications of rules in the real comprehension and use of a language. In real use the spoken words follow one another at the rate of several hundred a minute" (O'Connor and

Twaddell 1960, 4). But in chess, after a little practice the application of rules becomes quite automatic. We do not think of the rules at all until our opponent tries to violate them. It is "analogy" that requires puzzle-solving; rules need only to be followed, not puzzled out.

The empiricist argument that language is learned by conditioning and drill also seems to rest entirely on the premise that language use is automatic. But this does not follow, either. The general fallacy involved is pointed out by Scheffler in discussing an argument of Ryle's. He says,

> What is it that leads Ryle to say that facilities are built up by drill? Surely his reason must be that facilities are routinizable, becoming increasingly automatic as they are developed. This does *not* however, *at all* imply that drill alone is capable of building them up. Once they are developed, they are indeed automatic and repetitive; it cannot be inferred that they are therefore *acquired* in an automatic and repetitive way . . . "After the toddling-age," says Ryle, "we walk on pavements without minding our steps." But then during the toddling-age we *do* mind our steps, and drill is, at least at this stage, inappropriate (Scheffler 1965, 105).

This should be an obvious point: routine and automatic facilities are often built up slowly and painstakingly. A good typist can type almost as easily as he speaks, without thinking about what he is doing; but when he first learned to type he had to spell out each word and concentrate on where to place each finger. The same is true of language learning. In de Sauzé's words, there are "two stages of knowledge of a language: the 'conscious' one, during which we use the language slowly, applying rules of grammar, reasoning various relationships as we proceed. The second one, ... the 'automatic' stage, occurs when we speak, read, and write the language substantially like our mother tongue" (de Sauzé 1953, 14).

What does it mean to "learn" the rules of grammar that we apply so carefully when we first speak a foreign language? It does *not* mean to memorize the formulations of the rules from a grammar book. Let us take again the example of chess: the most efficient way to master the rules of chess would not be to memorize the official rule booklet. Instead, one should have a teacher who would show him how to move each piece, and how to castle, and how to* capture the opponent's pieces. The teacher would help him make the moves and would guide him through his first game. Rules for action are best learned in conjunction with demonstration and practice of the action. The particular formulation of the rules is not terribly important: the rules of chess could probably be explained by sign language alone. But suppose instead of explaining the rules you had a learner memorize some championship games: how much longer would it take for a person to figure out the simple moves that each piece can make! So it is with language. A few carefully chosen examples of a rule in operation can lead us to understand the rule. But embedding these examples in a dialog to be memorized might mask their significance entirely.

3. Man is uniquely built to learn languages

Perhaps the most striking phenomenon of language is its universality. Virtually every person in the world knows a language. Few other cultural phenomena are that universal. Equally noteworthy, perhaps, is the fact that lower animals cannot learn human language. A certain amount of communication is possible between man and animal, but it is not because the animals understand language. Try speaking to your dog in a foreign language—it will probably work as well as English. The universality of language learning would be a vacuous notion, of course, if it were true that "languages could differ from each other unpredictably and without limit" (cf. Joos 1958, 96). But languages are not all that different, and, indeed, on an abstract level all human languages have a similar design. All languages have sentences made up of words. They can all produce arbitrarily long sentences by embedding sentences within other sentences. They all exhibit grammatical relationships such as subject and predicate. The words in all languages are made up of discrete sound segments, and these discrete sounds can be sorted into natural classes according to their distinctive features (cf. Chomsky and Halle 1968). The similarities among all languages define human language as being qualitatively different from the so-called "animal languages," and they seem to be dependent on the biological make-up of man.

Eric Lenneberg (1967) has the most detailed discussion of *The Biological Foundations of Language*. He points out that human beings can overcome tremendous handicaps to learn languages. Blind children learn languages as easily as seeing children do. Deaf children can learn language through writing. Normal children of nonspeaking deaf parents learn to speak with very little delay. As mentioned before, one child who was physically unable to articulate a single word learned nevertheless to understand English both in spoken and written form. People with very defective intellects are not prevented from learning language—so long as a person reaches a mental age of six by the time he is twelve years old, he can and will learn a language. But in spite of persistent efforts, no one has been able to teach a human language to a nonhuman animal.

It is not just the size of man's brain that allows him to learn language; it is the organization of his brain. Animals with small brains *can* learn language if they are human. Lenneberg has demonstrated this from the case of the so-called bird-headed dwarfs. These dwarfs have the same body proportions as normal adults, but they attain a mature height of only two or three feet. As adults, their head circumference and brain weight are those of a normal new-born infant. Yet they are able to master language at least as well as the normal five-year-old (Lenneberg 1967, 69-70).

Developmental studies of language learning are extremely important in showing the dependence of language learning on biological processes. The language development of every child is remarkably similar regardless of the language, culture, or particular home situation. Some children learn language sooner and faster than others, but the *order* of development is more or less the same for all children, even for retarded children, and is related to other parts of the maturation process (Lenneberg 1967). And there are some rather striking differences between the abilities of adults and children to learn languages.

Children begin learning language by naming. These first names are often very generalized categories. Lenneberg gives the examples that "car" might be used for all vehicles, "dog" for all animals, and "daddy" for all people. The child finds some phrase asking, "What's that?" and delights in manipulating its environment to find out various names. This first stage of language is limited to approximately fifty words or phrases of three syllables or less, and these elements are never combined. In English, the most common words of the language are the articles "a," "an," and "the" (they account for about 5 to 10 per cent of the words on a given page). But these words never appear among the first words of the child. Syntax is built up in later stages, following pretty much the same developmental pattern in all children. Color naming is a late phenomenon, as is the use of conditional and subjunctive verb phrases.

Children play around with their language, exercising it in both a poetic and metalingual fashion. They try to see what they can do with their language, even when no one is present to reinforce them in any manner. They do this when playing by themselves and when lying in bed before going to sleep (cf. Jespersen 1922, 131; Weir 1961).

The development of language continues throughout one's life, of course. College freshmen are capable of a great deal of grammatical refinement, as their professors will affirm. The vocabulary development of school children and college students is nothing short of phenomenal. Slang, added to all the technical and scientific vocabulary, amounts to several thousand words each year. Twelve year olds have a recognition vocabulary of about 135,000 words. Harvard freshmen know about 200,000 words. The typical thirty-year-old Ph.D. knows about 250,000 words. [10] The unabridged Webster's Third International Dictionary has 450,000 words. Vocabulary development continues in a natural, almost unnoticed fashion as long as one lives and is interested in new things.

---

[10]These estimates are based on my own testing of nearly 200 people, using a representative sample of words from Webster's Third. A fuller report of these findings is in preparation.

Is language learning something magic? Is it automatic upon mere exposure to speech? If I move to a foreign country, will the foreign language automatically grasp hold of my psyche and make me bilingual without any effort on my part? No, language learning is definitely not automatic, not even for children.[11]

Americans in foreign countries—both children and adults—frequently fail to learn the local language. In Montreal, children are continually exposed to two languages, but they usually learn only one. Montreal is said to be a city of two unilingualisms rather than a bilingual city. There are severe limitations to the kind of social situation that will result in language learning. And the same goes for the classroom situation—mere exposure to a foreign language either in the town or in the classroom is no guarantee that a person will learn the language.

Suppose you pipe radio Peking into your child's nursery twenty-four hours a day. Will he learn Chinese? No. Spoken language, like writing, requires a Rosetta stone. It is the *meaning* of words and sentences that is crucial to language learning. *Languages cannot be learned without a situation of meaningful use.* We can learn foreign languages wherever we can find people to talk with us in the language, to answer for us the child's questions "What's this?", "Why?", "What does that mean?" But being in the presence of a language is of little help unless we are as active as the child in learning a language, and unless we ask the same sorts of questions.

There is an old myth which says that adults can never be as good at learning languages as children are. Adults have to work at language learning, and, it is said, children do not. Adults inevitably have foreign accents, but children do not. Wilder Penfield suggested that this myth was true, and that it was due to the changes in the brain that occur at adolescence (Penfield 1953). But the maturation of the brain is not to the

---

[11] Surprisingly, a number of linguists associated with generative grammar, even including Lenneberg, have taken the opposing view that language acquisition in children is automatic upon mere exposure. Lenneberg calls this "resonance." I argue in some detail against the notion of resonance in my article, "Resonance and Language Learning." The paragraphs which follow are based on that discussion.

adult's disadvantage! The adult can reason more effectively than the child, and this fact actually allows him to learn foreign languages faster than children can. The child might possibly be superior in learning to pronounce, but both in vocabulary and grammar (the ability to say things), the adult is a superior learner. The problem is not that the adult is unable to get to the five-year-old language level as fast as the five-year-old can. The adult wants to get to an adult level in the foreign language as fast as the five-year-old gets to his own level. If educated adults have a vocabulary level of more than 200,000 words in their native language, it is asking a lot to want to become totally bilingual even in 1,000 hours of instruction.

Even in pronunciation, children are overrated as language learners. Language programs in the elementary schools have found out that children develop foreign accents and have to be taught to pronounce correctly, even when they have native speaker teachers to mimic. This is not surprising when we recall that children do not pronounce their own native languages very well at first; it takes quite a while for some children to shake off their "baby talk." Many immigrant children do not lose their foreign accents until after they have experienced the cruel ridicule of their peers. It is true that children are more capable of losing their accents than adults are, but the contrast is made greater because adults are frequently less willing to suppress their foreign accent. Peter Ustinov says that he has no accent when acting in a French movie, but that he cannot speak French without an accent in a face to face conversation. This is a natural phenomenon, because people realize that a foreign accent is their best passport, as Einar Haugen has said (Haugen 1965). Haugen relates the story of a girl from San Francisco who married a Frenchman. Her pronunciation was so perfect that her acquaintances in France thought she was a rather stupid and uncultured Frenchwoman instead of an exotic foreigner with an exceptionally good knowledge of French. Most adults prefer to retain their foreign identity and accent.

Except in bilingual localities, we cannot be confident that the earlier we start teaching a foreign language the better. In Cleveland they began teaching foreign languages in the elementary school to high I.Q. children in 1922. But after several years of experimentation they seemed to be of the opinion that the seventh grade was the optimum time to begin teaching a foreign language, largely because seventh graders could use their powers of reasoning so much more effectively than grade school children could (de Sauzé 1959, 70). In three semesters, junior high students can surpass the child with six years study in grade school. But high school students can get to the same point in two semesters, and college students in one semester. Maturity clearly helps one in learning languages faster.

We have been discussing the point that "man is uniquely built to learn languages." The upshot of the discussion is that man actually *learns* languages. Language habits are not just impressed upon us from the outside. But language learning is a very natural and almost effortless activity for the person endowed with curiosity; indeed, it is an activity which we carry on until our death. If foreign-language teachers can co-operate with this natural process, we can expect to have both a more enjoyable and a more effective classroom experience.

4. A living language is a language in which we can think

Take the example of a singer who sings a concert in faultless German without understanding a word. Or the Latin-American politician who reads a speech in perfect English only to resort to using an interpreter in the question and answer period. These people are using the speech of a foreign language to communicate. But being able to mimic or even to communicate does not mean in these cases that the person knows the language that he is using. We cannot say we know a language until we can think in it.

Thinking is not restricted to the use of language, of course. Lenneberg has shown that six-year-old deaf children who have not yet learned language have a very complex concept structure. On the Leiter International Performance Test, which tests nonverbal concepts and reasoning ability, deaf six-year-olds are able to perform as well as six-year-olds who know English (Lenneberg 1967, 357-363). But a large part of our abstract thinking is done with the use of language.

In arguing that the rules of grammar are "psychologically real," we have already indicated how bound up language use is to thinking. If a person has merely memorized the formulations of the rules from a grammar book, then the rules are not yet psychologically real and cannot be used for thinking, and the language remains dead for that person.

Thinking demands not just grammatical rules, it demands words. As soon as a scientist or philosopher invents a new concept he gives it a name so that he can handle it more easily in his thoughts. This is another aspect of how a language lives: it keeps growing—both in the absolute sense of new words being coined, and in the relative sense of each person learning new words all the time.

As we have seen above, it is not unusual for a twenty-five--year-old speaker of English to have a vocabulary of 200,000 words. This means that he has learned an average of more than twenty words every day that he has been alive. One might say that this feat of learning is aided by the tremendous redundancy of a language. Once we know *milk* and *man*, we have no trouble learning *milkman*. But we have to learn these compound words nevertheless, or else we would be predicting that a *gingerbread man* was the man who delivers gingerbread, and that a *milkmaid* was a feminine milkman. And the redundancy of language does not make it child's play to memorize an arbitrary list of twenty Greek words every day. The reason that we can remember vocabulary so easily in a living language is that each new word expresses for us a thought or it labels a concept which we want to remember. If the word is essential for the thought, we will remember the word. "Association is the fundamental law of memory, " says de Sauzé, "we must introduce [the student] very early to a text that expresses thought and not to a haphazard collection of sentences that jump from the cow to the moon and create in the mind of the student the distinct impression that the new language is not capable of conveying thought, but only serves to illustrate grammatical relationship" (de Sauzé 1959, 9-10).

No American had trouble learning *defoliation* during the 1964 presidential campaign. *Overkill* and *pre-emptive war* are bothersome concepts, but easy words. The whole world has learned the terminology of spacecraft and rocketry since 1957, so the driver's seat of the new Peugeot becomes the "command module." Vocabulary learning is an integral part of learning about new things and expressing new thoughts. But memorizing a dictionary does not work. The words are dead, and do not stand for any living concept or thought. Memorizing basic sentences or dialogs is not much better; still the language is basically dead, and the words are not our words, the thoughts not our thoughts.

In learning grammar, the same law of association holds in making the rules of grammar psychologically real and alive instead of letting them remain dead abstractions. Memorizing a grammatical rule ("invert subject and verb to make a question") will not give us a correct association for the grammatical processes involved.

The important thing about grammar is that changes in grammatical structure bring about changes in meaning. Unless we can link the structure to the meaning, there is no use in being able to produce the structure. To learn how to form the past tense of the verb, we talk about what we *did* yesterday. To learn the present perfect tense, we talk about what we *have done* in the last several weeks. With this kind of practice, grammar becomes a means of expressing our thoughts, and it becomes a living conception for us.[12]

Thus learning a living language involves learning to think in that language. *Meaningful practice* rather than drill is the only way this can come about. Guided practice in thinking (through speaking, writing, listening, or reading) is what enables a person to learn a living language in which he can think.

---

[12] The view of grammar learning presented here affirms that the technical apparatus of formal grammatical descriptions is irrelevant. We will discuss this point more fully in Chapter eight. But we might note here that when Chomsky spoke to language teachers on "Linguistic Theory" (1966b) he did not even mention such apparatus as phrase-structure rules and transformations. Almost all grammatical descriptions, even the best generative transformational grammars, fail to deal adequately with meaning. The language student is led to understand the rules of grammar from examples, and *to formulate the rules primarily in terms of the changes in meaning.*

CHAPTER 4

ON CHOOSING BETWEEN THE TWO THEORIES

To my satisfaction, and to that of a rapidly increasing number of other linguists, Chomsky's arguments in favor of the rationalist theory of language learning are convincing. Yet Chomsky has failed to convert a large number of prominent linguists who still remain committed to the empiricist presuppositions about science.

In choosing between the theories, the issue at stake, according to the rationalist, is an issue of fact: language is obviously a mental phenomenon and must be treated as such in our study of it. For the empiricist the issue at stake is "science": if language is going to be studied scientifically, then we must exclude all evidence about language except the observable overt linguistic behavior of other people.

Charles F. Hockett, the most outspoken and scornful critic of what he calls Chomsky's "antiscientific" position, has called Chomsky himself a "neomedieval philosopher" (Hockett 1967, 144). But then, of course, Hockett is also a neomedieval philosopher, an updated nominalist. This nominalism of the linguistic descriptivists has been expressed most explicitly by W. F. Twaddell:

Whatever our attitude toward. mind, spirit, soul, etc., as realities, we must agree that the scientist proceeds as though there were no such things, as though all his information were acquired through processes of his physiological nervous system. In so far as he occupies himself with psychical, non-material forces, the scientist is not a scientist. *The scientific method is quite simply the convention that mind does not exist: science adopts the nominalistic attitude toward the problem of the universals, in matters of procedure* (Twaddell 1935, 57, note 8, italics added).

The above comment of Twaddell's is a footnote to a paragraph which contains the following two propositions: "(1) we have no right to guess about the workings of an inaccessible 'mind,' and (2) we can secure no advantage from such guesses. The linguistic processes of the 'mind' as such are quite simply unobservable; and introspection about linguistic processes is notoriously a fire in a wooden stove" (Twaddell 1935, 57).

"Introspection" has been one of the focal points of the controversy. The rationalist would argue that the richest potential gold mine of linguistic information comes from our own knowledge of our native tongue. We can observe our own mental activity through thinking; we know we have "knowledge" of a language, and we know what we can and cannot do with the language. We know what is grammatical for us in a language, and what is ungrammatical. We can distinguish ungrammatical sentences from false ones or silly ones. Even if a sentence is meaningful, we know when it is ungrammatical (suppose the printer had just printed "it it ungrammatical"; almost every reader would have caught the mistake and gotten the intended meaning from this ungrammatical sentence). Indeed the rationalist would say that truly adequate grammars can be written only by linguists who have native or near native proficiency in the languages they describe. Most American generative grammarians, therefore, choose their native English as their object of study.

With a few notable exceptions, the descriptivists have tended to shy away from their native English because of the difficulty in being objective about their own language; they have chosen instead to go out to do field work on an American Indian language or some other language which they did not know well—or which indeed they sometimes never learn to speak at all.

It is really impossible to refute either one of these theories of language to the satisfaction of anyone who is deeply committed to the other theory. Chomsky can argue that the empiricists are ignoring crucial evidence about language and other mental phenomena by refusing to study these mental phenomena directly and by insisting on recognizing only the indirect evidence of other people's observable behavior. But this argument will not sway someone who is deeply committed to excluding the "misleading" evidence of introspection and thought. Charles Hockett's attempted refutation of Chomsky (Hockett 1968) is likewise irrelevant to someone who has accepted Chomsky's linguistic presuppositions.

Hockett's approach to refutation was to list nineteen propositions which summarize Chomsky's theory and then to have Chomsky himself edit and approve these propositions. The chief issue at stake, Hockett says, is whether language is a "well-defined" system of rules or an "ill-defined" system of habits. If we assume that language is not a well-defined system of rules, he states, we can then drop almost all the rest of Chomsky's propositions as being irrelevant. So far so good; he has surely hit upon the crucial issue.

The rationalists would have a well-defined system of rules which can generate infinitely many new grammatical sentences and which can rule out deviant utterances as being ungrammatical. The empiricists would say that language is an ill-defined system of habits which allows any new sentence produced by such flexible processes as analogy, blending, and editing, and which would not rule out any utterance as ungrammatical.

But then instead of refuting the proposition that a grammar is a well-defined system of rules, Hockett merely asserts that "there is no *obvious evidence* directly supporting this proposal" (Hockett 1968, 88, italics added). He has, of course, excluded the unobservable (not obvious) evidence of introspection and self-knowledge. Content with that, Hockett merely restates his belief that language is a system of observable habits, that it is not a matter of knowledge, and that language is used through processes of mimicry, analogy, blending, and editing. His criticism of Chomsky is convincing only to those who agree in excluding the evidence of introspection and thought.

Some wavering or uncommitted people get quite upset at the necessity of choosing between two theories. Sometimes they try the "mugwump" alternative, sitting on the fence and saying that both theories are exaggerations and that the truth lies in the middle. Both theories, after all, are talking about the same thing—language—so any differences must be terminological. F. W. Householder, for example, in reviewing Hockett's argument above, states: "Hockett's objection to C_3 is the use of 'know' where he would prefer to use the term 'habit.' Since this is simply a question of definition (Chomsky clearly uses 'know' in a sense for which Hockett, like many of us, does use 'have the habit of' or something similar), we can skip it" (Householder 1970, 132). That is grossly unfair to both Hockett and Chomsky. It is like saying that any theological differences between Quakers and Moslems are merely terminological, since both believe in God. In practice it makes a world of difference whether a linguist looks at language and sees a system of conditioned habits or a symbolic system which a person knows; whether he sees in language use a process of mimicry and analogy, or a process of rule-governed creativity. And one of the greatest practical differences between the theories lies in the language-teaching methodologies which they spawn.

As proof that interest can be maintained, one can point to the summer demonstration school in Cleveland. Students in the summer school come on a purely voluntary basis and study the foreign language for three consecutive hours every day during the heat of summer. Classes are often very large and ages are mixed within broad groupings (cf. Mulhauser 1956). Milton Barall, after observing these classes, remarked that "To any observer who has had experience in the teaching of foreign languages, the results obtained by the youngsters . . . are almost unbelievable. Of the greatest importance is the enthusiasm which the pupils exhibit at all times" (Barall 1949, 135). It is this same interest and enthusiasm of the student that helps make the Berlitz schools so popular and profitable.

From de Sauzé's point of view, as an administrator,

> The most potent result is the renewed enthusiasm of the French teachers. They have faith in themselves, in their work, in its tremendous possibilities. To many of them it has been a revelation of the joy that may be found in doing something worthwhile in a worthwhile way: something that brings as its reward the satisfaction of achievement. . . . This new method of teaching makes new demands upon our French teachers, but they meet those demands cheerfully and adequately, and they glean their reward from the bubbling enthusiasm that they see on the faces of those youths, opening their eyes wide to the marvels of that new world—the new language (de Sauzé 1929, 98-99).

Teachers as well as students find the direct method intrinsically interesting; it is a great deal of fun trying to communicate with people who do not know your language—especially when this communication is organized in such a way that it is successful.

Compare with this the attitude of those who recommend mim-mem and pattern drill. They warn teachers that "Drills are inherently unnatural, contrived examples of the use of language. . . . Humanizing these devices is left to the teacher. Unless the students are stimulated by variety, novelty, and a quick change of cues, they may be mouthing meaningless sentences and in this unwilling frame of mind, no learning takes place" (Dacanay 1963, 192-193).

Or like William Moulton, they recommend that elementary language teaching should be done by graduate students, since teaching of this sort is not rewarding enough to ask someone to spend his life doing it. As he says, "The employment of graduate students provides for a gradual but constant turnover, which is desirable on the theory that none but the most devoted should teach exclusively elementary language courses for more than a few years" (Moulton 1952, 45). Similarly, Mortimer Graves despaired of finding a highly qualified high school language teacher for mim-mem and pattern drill: "If he is willing to spend twenty or thirty hours a week employing such high qualifications in the incessant and boring, and unintellectual drill which is so imperative in language learning, there is something else wrong with him" (Graves 1963, 2-3).

One of the most striking differences, then, between the direct method and mim-mem/pattern drill, is that the direct method is inherently interesting, while mim-mem and pattern drill have to be made interesting by the teacher. It is fun to establish communication in a foreign language as the direct method has us do. But with mim-mem and pattern drill, communication in the foreign language is postponed until after a reliable set of habits has been drilled into the student. Drill is not very much fun; meaningful practice is.

But there is another kind of interest which we should distinguish—and here the mim-mem texts are usually as good as most direct method texts. Language lessons have content; when we talk, we talk about something. Talking itself may be intrinsically interesting, but the content of what we say ought to be interesting, too.

De Sauze tries to choose vocabulary that junior high students will want to use in conversation, but I am not sure that the readings in his elementary textbook are very imaginative. Berlitz chooses vocabulary that businessmen need, and his textbooks are also businesslike.

"Dullness is a besetting sin of most language textbooks" —that is the opinion of Einar Haugen, and surely of most

other language students as well. Haugen wished that he could
have collaborated with a truly skilled Norwegian dramatist in
writing his *Spoken Norwegian* (1947) (Haugen 1951, 150).
An adult who is learning a foreign language simply cannot be
treated like a child, and the content of his foreign-language
lessons ought to be as sophisticated, imaginative, and
worthwhile as possible. For beginning pianists, we have the
brilliant elementary piano pieces of Bela Bartok's *Mikrokosmos* which are suitable for the concert hall. But there is
very little in foreign-language textbooks that is enjoyable
reading to native speakers of the language.

But even if we have nothing comparable to Bartok's
Mikrokosmos, there are a number of new textbooks which
deserve an honorable mention for interesting content. Yvone
Lénard's *Parole et Pensée* (1965), for example, a direct
method text for college students, takes de Sauzé's methodology and adds to it a truly French cultural content—at least
in some parts of the book. Lénard is not content merely to
produce Americans who can speak French; she wants to
impart to these Americans an understanding of French
culture and the French mentality as well. Edited selections
from major French writers and poets are scattered throughout the book (along with a remarkable selection of French
paintings). Other recent books which attempt to accomplish
much the same thing for college students include Pucciani
and Hamel's *Langue et Langage* (1967), Traversa's *Parola e
Pensiero* (1967), and Pfister's *Deutsch durch Deutsch* (1968).
Lénard is also writing a series of textbooks for high school
(1969). These books are taking steps to make the direct
method not only intrinsically interesting, but also interesting
in content as well.

6. Exclusive use of the foreign language

The key to the high morale of students and teachers who
use the direct method is the fact that no language except the
foreign language is used in the classroom. The challenge of
establishing communication in a foreign language brings
continuing pleasure to both students and teachers—but the
challenge is lost and interest wanes if they are allowed to

revert to their native language every time they are stuck or every time there is something serious to communicate.

It is quite possible to establish this communication in the foreign language from the very first day, as we have seen, through careful ordering of vocabulary and grammar in step by step progression.

Exclusive use of the foreign language also gives the maximum amount of practice in thinking and communicating in the foreign language—and that, after all, is the goal of the language classroom.

PART III

METHODS
OF
LANGUAGE
LEARNING

CHAPTER 5

MIMICRY—MEMORIZATION AND PATTERN DRILL

Descriptive linguists since the end of the nineteenth century have been in remarkable agreement with regard to how their empiricist theory of language learning should be applied to the foreign language classroom. The methods have become more refined and sophisticated, perhaps, but in essence they can all be reduced to the notions of mimicry, memorization (the two combined to "mim-mem"), and pattern drill.[13]

Mim-mem and pattern drill are actually complementary methods which have not always appeared together. Palmer

---

[13] There is one apparent exception which is genuinely recent —programed instruction. Programed instruction has developed only since 1954, when B. F. Skinner wrote his article "The Science of Learning and the Art of Teaching." It is said that programed instruction is a direct application of operant conditioning to teaching methodology. Yet in practice many programs for foreign language learning use mimicry, memorization, and pattern drill as their teaching methodology, only presenting these methods in the new format of programed instruction (cf. Valdman 1964; Carroll 1963a, 1963b). It would seem, then, that programed instruction qualifies only as a "technique" for language teaching, and not really a "method."

called for both methods (Palmer 1917, 1921), and his *One Hundred Substitution Tables* (1916) is the best early example of pattern drills published for class use. But Bloomfield and the linguists who prepared the Army language manuals put overwhelming emphasis on mimicry and memorization and very little on pattern drill.

On the other hand, the Michigan English Language Institute materials (Lado and Fries 1958) put the whole emphasis on pattern drill with very little memorization of connected dialog or text. Mimicry is retained, of course, in all drills and especially in the pronunciation drills.

More recently, textbooks have again tried to balance the methods of mimicry, memorization, and pattern drill. A good example of this is *Modern Spanish* (Bolinger et al. 1960; second edition 1966). This is a textbook prepared by a committee of six authors under the auspices of the Modern Language Association with a grant from the Rockefeller Foundation. This textbook, as a group project of the language teaching profession, is perhaps the most carefully prepared and, methodologically, the most nicely balanced textbook within the empiricist approach. Except for Unit One, each of the twenty-four units in *Modern Spanish* has three parts. The first part contains a twenty-five to thirty sentence dialog which, it is insisted, must be memorized by the students. An idiomatic English translation is presented in parallel columns to the dialog. The second part, the major part of each unit, contains the pattern drills, based on words and constructions introduced in the dialogs. Memorization of the dialogs will facilitate going through the drills, however it is not expected that the teacher will have time to cover all the drills given him—the teacher chooses his drills from an embarrassment of riches. Very extensive grammatical explanations are presented in this part of the unit, but it is expected that the student will read this material at home after he has mastered the grammatical points through dialog memorization and drill. The third part of the unit contains a reading passage in which the same vocabulary and structure are reviewed once more.

To get the flavor of the kind of material which is to be memorized, here is an example of a dialog for memorization from a language we all know well—English. It is from *Modern English* (Rutherford 1968, 43).

Table 1. A Dialog for Memorization from an Intermediate
Level Textbook for English as a Foreign Language

Singh	I brought my I.D. card to the Housing Office.
Ram	Why on earth did you go there?
Singh	A couple of my books were missing. Somebody found them and took them there.
Ram	Were the people in the office very helpful?
Singh	Yes. Speaking of books, there aren't any more economics texts on the shelves.
Ram	I know. I stood in line and bought one of the last copies. New.
Singh	Yes. The cheap used copies went fast. But you can't save money that way.
Ram	Well, I'm applying for a student loan.
Singh	A loan for next semester? Whose idea was that?
Ram	It came from the Foreign Student Advisor. I can repay some of the money with a summer job.
Singh	What about right now? Are you short of cash?
Ram	No, thanks just the same. Next month there'll be a check in the mail from my government.

It is no mean feat to memorize such a dialog—even if English is your native tongue. It jumps from I.D. cards to the housing office, to books, to helpful people, to economics textbooks, to the cost of living, to student loans, to summer jobs, and to government checks. But presumably the student who learns this dialog will also learn some new idioms ("why on earth . . . ?", "Are you short of cash?", "speaking of books . . . ," etc.).

To understand about pattern drills, the best procedure, again, is to see some examples. Fe R. Dacanay (1963) gives examples of eighty different kinds of pattern drills, which she

reduces to four types: substitution drills, tranformation
drills, response drills, and translation drills (Dacanay 1963,
107 ff.).[14]

Let us examine six of Dacanay's eighty examples:

1)   "Simple substitution of intonation pattern

    Hè's alreâdy hére.↓   Hè's alreâdy hére?↑

    Shè's jûst arríved.↓   Shè's jûst arríved?↑

    Thèy nêver cáme.↓   Thèy nêver cáme?↑

    etc." (p. 113).

2)   Correlative substitution drill: "pronoun-antecedent agreement

I looked for the bag, but I couldn't find it.	I looked for the bag, but I couldn't find it.
———— book ————	I looked for the book, but I couldn't find it.
———— pen ————	I looked for the pen, but I couldn't find it.
———— twins ————	I looked for the twins, but I couldn't find them.
———— letters ————	I looked for the letters, but I couldn't find them.
———— receptionist –	I looked for the receptionist, but I couldn't find her.

etc." (p. 114).

---

[14] All four types are discussed by Palmer (1916, 1917, 1921)–though
he uses the term "conversion" instead of "transformation."

3) Moving slot substitution drill: "s-form of the verb and the present progressive construction expressing future time, possessives, adverbial expressions, etc.

The train leaves tomorrow at seven.	The train leaves tomorrow at seven.
——tonight ————————	The train leaves tonight at seven.
—bus —————————	The bus leaves tonight at seven.
————————— ten.	The bus leaves tonight at ten.
Our ————————————	Our bus leaves tonight at ten.
——guest ———————	Our guest leaves tonight at ten.
———————— Monday —	Our guest leaves Monday at ten.
————————is leaving ———	Our guest is leaving Monday at ten.
—— boat ———————	Our boat is leaving Monday at ten.
————————————noon.	Our boat is leaving Monday at noon.
My ———————————	My boat is leaving Monday at noon.
—— friend ————————	My friend is leaving Monday at noon.
——————left ———	My friend left Monday at noon."

(p. 116).

4) Transformation drill "Changing statements to questions

Teacher	Pupils
The girl is ready.	Is the girl ready?
The boy is coming.	Is the boy coming?
The others are here.	Are the others here?
The car has come.	Has the car come?
The teacher can go.	Can the teacher go?
The students can wait.	Can the students wait?

etc." (p. 117).

5)   Transformation expansion drill.

"The napkins are on the table.	The napkins are on the table.
paper	The paper napkins are on the table.
yellow	The yellow paper napkins are on the table.
pretty	The pretty yellow paper napkins are on the table.
two	The two pretty yellow paper napkins are on the table."

(p. 120).

6)   Response drill "with a cued alternate expression

Teacher	Student I	Cue	Student II
Are you going to the movies?	Are you going to the movies?	(zoo)	No, I'm going to the zoo.
— she ————	Is she going to the movies?	(dance)	No, she's going to the dance.
— he ————	Is he going to the movies?	(gym)	No, he's going to the gym.
—in the furniture business?	Is he in the furniture business?	(mining)	No, he's in the mining business.
— they ————	Are they in the furniture business?	(dry goods)	No, they're in the dry goods business.
———— summer school	Are they in summer school?	(taking a vacation)	No, they're taking a vacation."

(p. 144).

These drills involve nothing more than the manipulation of structures. There is no pretense that they do anything else; they are not intended to resemble real communication. For the drill which substitutes intonation patterns (example 1, above), it is not even necessary that the student know the meaning of the sentence he is working with. When questions are asked, as in the response drills (example 6, above), answers are put into the student's mouth. Dacanay explicitly sets "drill activity" over against "free communication activity" (p. 173).

The heavy emphasis on manipulating pattern drills is in large measure the result of a fear that the student will make mistakes. Since language learning is thought of as a habit-forming process, it cannot be held that students are able to learn from their mistakes. An incorrect response is seen as the beginning of an incorrect habit. Palmer expressed this fear of error as "The principle of accuracy: Do not allow the student to have opportunities for inaccurate work until he has arrived at the stage at which accurate work is to be reasonably expected" (Palmer 1921, 110). Jespersen, who had more sense than some of his colleagues in the empiricist camp, quoted with approval the Slavic proverb that "whoever wants to speak well must murder the language" (Jespersen 1904, 122). Palmer retorted that "In opposition to the principle of accuracy, we are frequently told that 'It is only by making mistakes that we learn not to make them,' and that 'Only by going into the water can we learn to swim.' These are cheap proverbs, and we may easily coin others such as: 'It is by making mistakes that we form the habit of making them'; or, 'He who has not learnt to swim will drown when thrown into deep water'" (Palmer 1921, 110-111).

Recently this point of view of Palmer's has been expressed very clearly in the teachers' materials for the "Aural-Oral Sequences" of Holt, Rinehart and Winston, Inc., a series of textbooks of which W. Freeman Twaddell is the general editorial advisor. These textbooks cover elementary and high school levels of instruction in German, French, and Spanish, using identical format for the three languages, and a nearly identical set of teachers' instructions.[15] This is a very orthodox and sophisticated series of textbooks, from an empiricist point of view, and Twaddell is explicit in stating the presuppositions for his methods. The most important thing about language learning is that it is habit formation, he argues, and there are five stages in the process of building up these habits: 1) Recognition, 2) Imitation, 3) Repetition, 4) Variation, and 5) Selection. *Recognition* involves perception and recognition of the structure and meaning of an utterance. *Imitation* is the mimicking of the sentence by the student immediately after the sentence is pronounced by the teacher or by the recording. *Repetition* is the recitation of the sentence by memory. In the first-year high school German textbook, there are 400 basic sentences which must be memorized. In addition, there is question-answer practice in which the answers are taken practically word for word from the basic sentences (Rehder et al. 1962a). *Variation* involves pattern drills of the types discussed above. And *selection* is the process by which the student "selects the appropriate sentence from his repertory to fit his need" (Twaddell et al. 1964b, 7). Note that even in "selection" there is no need of constructing new sentences according to a system of generative rules; the speaker is presumed to have a repertory of sentences made up of basic sentences which he has memorized in the "repetition" stage, along with sentences formed by analogy in the "variation" stage. "Selection" is merely the choosing of one of these already learned sentences.

It follows, in this view, that there should not be much practice of selection until the student has a well-established set of sentences from which he can select appropriate utterances. The elementary level of language instruction, then, emphasizes "imitation," "repetition," and "variation" (that is, mimicry, memorization, and pattern drill). Not until the second level of instruction does one emphasize "recog-

---

[15]See Rehder et al. 1962a, 1962b, 1963b, 1964, 1965, 1966; Bauer et al. 1964b; Côté et al. 1962; Keesee et al. 1964; La Grone et al. 1962.

nition" and "selection" (cf. Twaddell 1963; and O'Connor and Twaddell 1960). As Twaddell puts it, "Premature practice of selection would lead to mistakes or at best to hesitation or fumbling, which are directly contrary to the goal of forming correct firmly-established habits..." (Twaddell et al. 1964b, 7).

The doctrine that "language is a set of habits," then, dictates that one should avoid any real communication until after the set of habits is established correctly.

It should be noticed in the quotation above, that "hesitation and fumbling" are to be avoided as much as mistakes are. For that reason, the mimicking and the repeating of sentences by memory must be done at the normal speed of a native speaker who talks rather fast. This is a general tenet of all who use mimicry-memorization, and it leads to such techniques as the "backward build-up" (in which the student goes through "semester," "last semester," "the university last semester," and "attended the university last semester" in order to arrive at "Mr. Smith attended the university last semester"). Another technique to get the student to mimic correctly without hesitation and fumbling is to start the mimicry in chorus—first with the whole class, then half the class, then a single row, then finally mimicry by an individual student. It becomes a part of a "shaping" technique in which a student is not inhibited by his first incorrect attempts at mimcry.

School administrators might appreciate one feature of mim-mem and pattern drill methods—a feature which has no doubt contributed to the widespread adoption of this method: it is not necessary or even desirable that the teacher be competent in the language he teaches—at least not when he is teaching on the elementary level of instruction. As Twaddell and his colleagues state it in the teachers manual to their first year German textbook:

This oral practice is very different from a "direct method" or "conversational" approach which would demand of the teacher the kind of conversational fluency that comes only with long and continuing experience.... What is needed for the course is *oral accuracy*, the ability to pronounce correctly and with the proper grammar just those sentences and constructions which the pupils are learning and practicing (this "Manual" and the text materials are built up so that in the very process of directing the students' practice the teacher's own control of those sentences and constructions is reinforced and confirmed). Teachers with exceptional conversational fluency will have to restrain themselves to keep within that part of the German language which their students are to practice (Rehder et al. 1962a, xix).

If all a teacher needs is oral accuracy, why is a teacher necessary? Albert Valdman (1964) has asked this question in all seriousness. The oral accuracy of a machine will be better than that of most teachers, and the machine has the patience to repeat utterances indefinitely many times. Valdman argues that as long as audio-lingual methods are limited to mimicry, memorization, and pattern drill, the machine—properly programed—can take over. Valdman does not argue that this is better for the student than having a skilled teacher who uses methods involving real communication instead of mim-mem and pattern drill. Yet, he says, in the absence of large numbers of such skilled teachers, "the machine indeed will take over," even if the language instruction which results is not what we might desire (Valdman 1964, 34-35).

But on the other hand, Dacanay maintains that the teacher is very important in a drill-centered method, because, as she says,

Drills are inherently unnatural, contrived examples of the use of language. This disadvantage can be partially overcome if naturalness of expression, sequence, and situation are successfully re-created, with an attempt to intensify the experience as an alternative to the vividness of actual participation in real situations. This requires the exercise of imagination on the part of both teachers and students, though the initiative here, as always, lies on the teacher. A sparkling presentation will enhance any drill .... Humanizing these devices is left to the teacher. Unless the students are stimulated by variety, novelty, and a quick change of cues, they may be mouthing meaningless sentences and in this unwilling frame of mind, no learning takes place (Dacanay 1963, 192-193).

It will be noticed that the discussion of this method has concentrated almost wholly on elementary language instruction. Advanced instruction is for students who have reached what Twaddell calls "the post-learning stage" (Twaddell et al. 1964b, 7). The student has already acquired the structural habits of his new language, and he can concentrate on enlarging his vocabulary just as he does with his native language at school.

Mimicry, memorization, and pattern drill provide a thoroughgoing method of applying the empiricist theory of language learning to the classroom. It is designed precisely for a world in which language use is nothing but mimicry and analogy. Its greatest strength lies in its emphasis on the spoken aspect of language ("Language is speech, not writing"), and it gets excellent results in the teaching of pronunciation.

If students think this method insults their intelligence, they can be comforted that it is a very principled insult. Descriptivists cannot admit that the "mind" exists—either in the abstract or in their students. That would not be scientifically respectable. They chide the teachers who think that language is rule-governed and who tell their students to "Think, please!" in formulating their sentences (Mathieu 1964, 20).

Pattern drills require the students to pay attention only to the mechanics of manipulating grammatical structures. They are not required to think in the language when they do pattern drills. The meanings of the sentences are not very important, and the changes in meaning brought about by the drill make little impresson on the student's mind.

Bowen and Stockwell acknowledge that "The most difficult transition in learning a language is going from mechanical skill in reproducing patterns acquired by repetition to the construction of novel but appropriate sentences in natural social contexts" (foreword to Rutherford 1968, vii). *That is to say that mim-mem and pattern drill alone are not sufficient for language learning.* Students who have acquired these mechanical speech habits are still unable to think in the foreign language or to speak it in natural social contexts. After all this drill, students still need meaningful practice. Maybe all this drill is irrelevant in the first place. If mim-mem and pattern drills do not instill a living conception of grammar, maybe we should replace them with activities that do.

CHAPTER 6

FRANCOIS GOUIN AND THE SERIES METHOD

A century ago, François Gouin went off to Hamburg to learn German. He had been a Latin teacher while a university student in France and he thought that the quickest way to master German would be to memorize a German grammar book and a table of the 248 irregular German verbs. It took him only ten days of concentrated effort to do this in the isolation of his room. Proud of his accomplishment he hurried to the academy to test his new power in German. "But alas!", he writes, "in vain did I strain my ears; in vain my eye strove to interpret the slightest movements of the lips of the professor; in vain I passed from the first class room to a second; not a word, not a single word would penetrate to my understanding. Nay, more than this, I did not even distinguish a single one of the grammatical forms so newly studied; I did not recognize even a single one of the irregular verbs just freshly learnt, though they must certainly have fallen in crowds from the lips of the speaker" (Gouin 1880, 11).

This failure crushed him only for a moment. He had not yet lost faith in his classical method. In learning Greek he had "ten times learnt, ten times forgotten, and ten times more reconquered" Lancelot's *Garden of Greek Roots* (p. 12).

Perhaps what he needed now was a similar mastery over the German roots. It took him eight days to memorize the 800 roots and to digest again the grammar book and 248 irregular verbs. This time, he says, "I thought I really possessed the foundations of the language, as well as the laws and the secret of its forms, regular and irregular" (p. 13). But the result was the same as before: at the academy he understood not one word.

Up to this time he had isolated himself from the people around him and he thought now that he should try to learn the language through making conversation. He lived with a hairdresser, and he tried to listen to the conversation of the customers. Occasionally he pronounced a carefully prepared sentence, constructed with the aid of his roots and grammar, but these sentences always caused the customers to laugh. This process of language learning was very painful, and did not seem very effective. So he returned to his books in solitude.

Back to the classical method, he began translating Goethe and Schiller with the aid of a dictionary. But after eight days, he had been able to translate only eight pages, and he began again to question the classical method.

In a bookshop, Gouin found the fifty-fourth edition of a very popular book by Ollendorf, promising to teach German in ninety lessons. This book presented the language in terms of basic sentences, with a more or less inductive presentation of grammar. It contained dialogues of the following sort: "Have you any shoes?" "Yes, I have some shoes" (p. 19). Gouin isolated himself from all company for three weeks to master this book; but it was to no avail.

"There still remained one last method," Gouin tells us, "but one so strange, so extraordinary, so unusual—I might say, so heroic—that I hardly dared propose it to myself. This supreme means was nothing else than to learn off the whole dictionary" (p. 26-27). This he did. He learned 30,000 words in 30 days. Let us allow Gouin to tell us the results:

> The third week gave me the third quarter of the dictionary; the thirtieth day I turned page 314, the last; and more triumphant than Caesar, I exclaimed, "Vici!" That same evening I went to seek my crown at the university—a crown surely well merited.

To comprehend what now happened to me it is necessary to have studied profoundly, as I have since been able to do, the question of language; to have determined accurately the conditions in which mankind, infant or adult, must be placed that they may be able to learn any language, no matter which.

I understood not a word—not a single word! . . . And I permit no one to doubt the sincerity of this statement. "Not a word—not one single word" (pp. 30-31).

Unable to accept this verdict, he tried reading again, and it took him a day and a half to decipher two or three pages. He then decided that he must have forgotten part of the dictionary, and he went through it again for another month. This time he repeated on the second day all he had learned on the first, and so on, until on the thirtieth day he was able to repeat the entire dictionary. But then his eyes gave out; and the doctor forced him to remain blind for a month. This was long enough time for him to forget his vocabulary, so upon recovering his eyesight he memorized the dictionary a third time, and began the practice of reciting one seventh of it each day. But all this effort was of no help, and soon the summer holidays arrived. He returned home to France not being able to speak or understand German in spite of the fact that he had memorized the grammar, roots, and dictionary of the language. He had isolated himself in his room and had reduced the classical method of language learning to absurdity.

1. The discovery of the Series Method

When Gouin returned home for the summer vacation, he discovered that while he was gone his three-year-old nephew had learned to speak French. It was rather embarrassing to discover that the three-year-old had succeeded so easily in a task which Gouin had found impossible in spite of much effort. So Gouin spent the summer trying to discover the way in which the three-year-old learns a language.

One day the child made his first visit to a mill with his mother. Gouin describes how the child "went over the mill from top to bottom. He wanted to see everything, to hear the name of everything, to understand about everything. Everything had to be explained to him. . . . He curiously examined the bolters, the millstones, the hoppers. He made the men open the flour-store; he pulled back the curtain of the bran-room, admired the turning of the pans and belts, gazed with a sort of dread at the rotation of the shafting and the gearing of the cog-wheels . . ." (p. 36).

For an hour after his return home, the child was silent, digesting this experience in his mind. Then he began step by step telling everybody what had happened. Each time he told the story it was slightly different—he would forget details and go back to put them in. But each time he would pass, as Gouin puts it, "from fact to fact, from phrase to phrase, by the same familiar transition, 'and then . . . and then . . .' "(p. 37). The child insisted that Gouin make a water wheel on the small stream near by, and he insisted that his mother make him some small flour sacks. Then he went to his little mill and re-enacted his whole story, filling the bags with sand and telling everyone what he was doing, and repeating it aloud to himself if no one was listening.

It became evident to Gouin that language learning was primarily a matter of transforming perceptions into conceptions. The child used language to represent for himself the experience he had at the mill. When he visited the mill, he "perceived" a new phenomenon. When he returned home he digested this experience for an hour and then repeated the story of his experience over and over again in terms of his linguistic "conception" of the mill.

Language, then, is not so much an arbitrary set of conventions to be used for communication as it is a means of thinking, of representing the world to oneself. Language acquisition is not a conditioning process in which a person acquires the habit of saying certain things in certain situations; rather, it is a process in which the learner actively goes about trying to organize his perceptions of the world in terms of linguistic concepts.

How different this is from learning isolated words from a dictionary. Such words are not representations of reality or of any of the learner's perceptions; they are not living conceptions, but are dead abstractions. As Gouin said about his dictionary memorizing, "The word was always as a dead body stretched upon the paper. Its meaning shone not forth under my gaze; I could draw forth neither the idea nor the life. 'Tragen,' for instance, was for me but an arbitrary assemblage of six letters, perfectly incapable of revealing to me the effort or the special movement it had the mission to represent" (p. 16).

The direct representation of an experience into a linguistic conception is what distinguishes a "direct method" of language teaching from such "indirect" ones as the grammar-translation method and mim-mem, both of which rely on translation into another language for the understanding of the meaning of an utterance. It is this direct thinking in a language which makes it a living language.

Besides giving Gouin this insight into the purpose of a living language, the experience at the mill also taught him two of the "secrets of the child's memory." Gouin noticed that his nephew organized his concepts in terms of succession in time and in terms of ends and means. In describing the activities of the mill, the child always used the same order. Gouin seized upon this idea as the basis for his methodology: concepts are naturally ordered in *series*. Students will learn a foreign language more quickly and remember it more easily if they are presented with descriptions of these natural series. So, for example, in the first lesson of a foreign language we would learn this series:

—I walk towards the door,	I walk
I draw near to the door.	I draw near
I draw nearer to the door.	I draw nearer
I get to the door.	I get to
I stop at the door.	I stop
—I stretch out my arm.	I stretch out
I take hold of the handle.	I take hold
I turn the handle.	I turn
I open the door.	I open
I pull the door.	I pull
—The door moves,	moves
the door turns on its hinges,	turns
the door turns and turns,	turns
I open the door wide,	I open
I let go the handle.	I let go

(pp. 129-130).

This series of fifteen sentences is so easy to remember that many people can repeat it verbatim in their native language after reading it through only once. That is a remarkable insight into memory. For we all know that if these fifteen sentences were shuffled around and presented in some random order, few people could repeat them in the same random order after one reading.

For insight into memory, Gouin was way ahead of present-day psycholinguists. George Miller and his colleagues have shown in various experiments that words are perceived and remembered more easily when presented in the context of grammatical sentences (cf. G. A. Miller 1962, 1964a). It was this finding that caused Miller to suggest that sentences are perceived more in terms of their larger constituents than in terms of their phonemes or morphemes. He makes the comment that "As long as we studied speech perception in terms of lists of words spoken in isolation, the existence of these larger units was not apparent" (G. A. Miller 1962, 754). For insight into memory, psycholinguists who deal with sentences are a step farther than those who deal with lists of "paired associates." But Gouin was a step farther than either of these by working within series of sentences.

Gouin's claim is actually stronger than the assertion that a natural series of sentences is easy to remember. He claims that a child will naturally order his concepts in terms of sequence in time and means-end relationships, even if the perceptions do not come to him in that order. Frequently the child will notice events without noticing their cause, and then he will have to search out the causes, the means to the end.

There was also a second insight into memory—"incubation." Gouin noticed that it takes a few days for a new concept or expression of language to settle itself in the memory. A language learner, then, must be careful to use his newly acquired words and rules rather frequently for a few days before he lets them repose in his memory—he must use them at least in thinking if not in speaking or understanding. Apparently recent studies in the biochemistry of the brain suggest that there is a physiological correlate to this "incubation" in the length of time it takes for synthesis of RNA after a learning experience—the presumption being that the new knowledge is coded biochemically (cf. Haydén 1967).

One final observation from the experience at the mill: children learn languages in sentences, with the verb being the most crucial constituent. It will be noticed in the exercise about opening the door, quoted above, that the verbs were listed separately beside each sentence. One of Gouin's techniques was to have his students repeat the exercise looking only at the column of verbs. The emphasis on the verb was inspired by the three-year-old's emphasis on it; further, it fits well with the ordering of things in succession of time. As Gouin puts it, "The German term 'Zeit-wort' (verb, or 'time-word') is a whole chapter of psychology. In time and by time everything is in order, because everything in it is successive, everything springs from something else. The method which rests upon the verb is therefore based upon a principle of order" (p. 46). Perhaps there were also syntactic reasons why the smphasis on the verb was so fruitful for Gouin. Chomsky has noted, for example, that in a generative grammar the lexical phrase marker is more complex for the verb than for the noun. The verb must be categorized in terms of the syntactic contexts in which it can appear. A transitive verb, for example, must be marked that it appears only before an object noun phrase. Nouns, on the other hand, are not categorized in terms of the verb contexts in which they appear; they need only the subcategorization in terms of their inherent features (cf. Chomsky 1965, chapter 2).

2. The Series Method

Gouin had very high goals as a language teacher. He wanted to translate the "whole individuality" of his students into the new language and thereby make them truly bilingual. His curriculum, then, would have to mirror the entire experience of the student. This could be accomplished, Gouin estimated, in a book of 4,000 pages, with one exercise on each page. The course would be organized around facts concerning the man, the quadruped, the bird, the reptile, the insect, the plant, and the elements. Each of these would have several subdivisions, or general series. For example, the man gives us the series of the child, the student, the young man, mature age, the trades, the arts, and so forth. The elements give the series of the river, the sea, the storm, the sun, and so on (pp. 61-62).

In order to see how the various exercises are related, let us examine two exercises from the series of the stove:

I. The girl chops some wood.

—The girl goes and seeks a piece of wood,	goes and seeks
she takes a hatchet,	takes
she draws near to the block.	draws near
she places the wood on this block.	places
she raises the hatchet,	raises
she brings down the hatchet,	brings down
the blade strikes against the wood,	strikes against
the blade penetrates the wood,	penetrates
the blade cleaves the wood,	cleaves
the pieces fall right and left.	fall
—The girl picks up one of the pieces,	picks up
places it upon the block,	places
raises her hatchet,	raises
brings down her hatchet,	brings down
and chops the piece of wood,	chops
she chops another piece, and then another,	chops
she chops up all the wood.	chops
—She puts down her hatchet,	puts down
gathers up the pieces into her apron,	gathers up
takes one or two logs and some shavings,	takes
and carries them to the stove.	carries

II. The girl lights the stove.

—She puts down the wood in front of the stove,	puts down
she crouches down in front of the stove,	crouches down
she opens the door of the stove,	opens

she removes the ashes,	removes
she cleans out the stove,	cleans out
she puts in the shavings first,	puts in
then she puts in the chopped firewood on top of these,	puts in
and she places the logs upon the firewood.	places

—This done,	done
she takes a match,	takes
strikes the match,	strikes
lights the match,	lights
puts the light to the shavings,	puts
and closes the stove-door.	closes

—The fire is communicated to the firewood,	is communicated
the firewood blazes;	blazes
the fire is communicated to the logs,	is communicated
the logs burn,	burn
the flames rush up the stove-pipe,	rush up
the stove roars.	roars

—The smoke escapes up the stove-pipe,	escapes
the stove-pipe gets hot,	gets hot
the stove gets hot,	gets hot
and radiates heat all over the room	radiates

(pp. 120-121).

Gouin found that the practical limit for each exercise was from twenty-two to twenty-five sentences. If kept to that length, the series—with their own intrinsic organization—were so easy to learn that, on the average, he says, five exercises could be assimilated in one hour. And after one sixth of the curriculum was finished, the exercises could be assimilated twelve to an hour (pp. 294-295).

Besides the language of objective facts which is presented in the series, there is another aspect of language which is learned through classroom conversation interspersed throughout the exercise. This is what Gouin calls the "subjective language." As an example we have this recitation which looks almost absurd when written down, but may not have been quite so absurd in actual practice:

Teacher.—Here is a door: to open it, what is it you do?
Pupil.—First of all, I walk towards the door.
Teacher.—Capital! And then what do you do?
Pupil.—I draw nearer to the door.
Teacher.—Capital! And then what do you do?
Pupil.—I get to the door.
Teacher.—Capital! And then what do you do?
Pupil.—I stop at the door.
Teacher.—Capital! And then what do you do?
Pupil.—I stretch out my arm.
Teacher.—Capital! And then what do you do?
Pupil.—I take hold of the handle.
Teacher.—Capital! And then what do you do next?
Pupil.—I turn the handle.
Teacher.—Capital! And what do you do after that?
Pupil.—I pull the door.
Teacher.—Capital! And then what happens?
Pupil.—The door moves.
Teacher.—Capital! And after that what happens?
Pupil.—The door turns on its hinges.
Teacher.—Capital! And then what do you do?
Pupil.—I leave go the handle.
Teacher.—Capital! The aim is attained and the lesson finished (p. 160).

An exercise of this sort sounds better in a foreign language, perhaps—"A merveille! Et puis? . . ." But Gouin makes this comment not much of an overstatement: "Now, I would ask, Has this locution, 'Capital!' [A merveille!] by the effect of this exercise, entered into the pupil's memory? If you doubt it, try the experiment. This expression is not only in his memory—it is part of his very nature, and is there for ever" (p. 161). And what Gouin has done with this one expression. he promises to do with thousands of other expressions in the subjective language.

One of the features of the series system is that it easily allows the students to take the part of the teacher in conducting the exercises. In this way the students get practice in saying "Capital!" and other phrases of the subjective language.

After the exercises have been learned orally, Gouin has his students write out the exercises either from memory or from looking only at the column of verbs. This has the effect of providing a change of pace in the classroom while reviewing the lesson and teaching the student to write. Everything which the student can say, he can write. But the series method does not provide for any reading from ordinary texts—only the series exercises themselves are read. After the basic series are mastered, however, Gouin presents classics of literature to be read in series format. Thus he gives, for example, a fable of La Fontaine transcribed as two series exercises. It is the format which is changed, not the actual fable. Each clause appears on a single line with the verb isolated in a separate column. When the pupil reconstructs the fable with the aid of the column of verbs, he is not repeating it by rote; he is recreating it "with his judgment" (p. 330). He is thus making the masterpiece his own "by conceiving it in his mind." He is teaching himself to write in much the same way that Benjamin Franklin taught himself to write by reconstructing the essays from *The Spectator*. Gouin uses this technique with literature, particularly in Latin, with classics such as Vergil's *Aeneid*, but also in other languages with history and the sciences as well as with literary masterpieces. But all these "auxiliary series" presuppose that the student has already mastered the ordinary series of the language, and has already learned the language which is being studied. The reading of connected prose, then, is postponed to a very advanced stage of instruction.

3. Grammar in the Series Method

As for grammar, Gouin shared the view of other traditional grammarians that language was rule-governed behavior. But he did not believe that grammar should be taught in terms of abstract rules and paradigms as it was in the classical method. He was not against grammar, but merely the manner in which it was taught. Instead of showing the student the conjugation written out on paper, Gouin wanted to write the conjugation "not upon paper, but on the thought," so that he would be "forming of the conjugation a 'conception' " (p. 206). As he says,

The grammar of childhood is indeed a grammar of intuition; but this intuition—let no one be deceived upon this point—is the result of a prodigious labour . . . our method does not in reality propose any less aim than to discover, or rather to reveal, the mysterious process which creates this intuition, and endows the human mind with its power. Therefore, if we wish to speak a language with the surety and quickness of the child, we must pass through the apprenticeship that he passes through. There is therefore a process to be followed; there is something to learn, something to be studied. We are, therefore, in accord, at least so far as regards the basis, with those who maintain that a language cannot be learnt without learning rules. On the other hand, we have clearly demonstrated that there is only one road that leads to intuition, that which goes from the abstract to the concrete, from the general to the particular, from the imaginary to the real (pp. 210-211).

Grammar is taught by means of the series, so that in the process of learning the series, one acquires the grammar as well. For example, the conjugation of the verb begins with the first lesson. Gouin discourages running through conjugations in the manner "I walk towards the door; thou walkest towards the door; he walks towards the door," etc. Instead, he has the student put the whole exercise into a different person: "he walks towards the door, he draws near to the door, he comes to the door," etc. Likewise, tense can be introduced by asking the student, "Yesterday what did you do?" And we get the answer, "Yesterday I walked towards the door, I drew near to the door, I came to the door," etc. Gouin points out that "owing to the nature and organization of our exercises, we conjugate one after the other some fifteen or twenty verbs, without allowing any one of them to appear under the form of an abstraction. Few books, assuredly, can offer this advantage: 'to force the pupil to think of an actual thing, to represent real facts while conjugating verbs' " (p. 202).

4. Strengths and Weaknesses of the Series Method

Gouin had a very ambitious program for language learning. He estimated that a language could be learned in from 800 to 900 hours of instruction, with no homework. At that time the student would be truly bilingual, and would have translated his whole individuality into the new language. The 4,000 exercises presented would contain enough words for a medium-sized dictionary, and each of these words would be in a context which forced the student to think of the reality represented by the word. The natural series provide a kind of meaningful practice which enables a student to remember a fantastic amount of language after a relatively short exposure. We have an impartial observation that the method actually worked very well (Brekke 1894). Yet there are many methodological flaws in the series system—flaws which would seem to preclude our taking over Gouin's method in the exact form he left it.

Linguists in the empiricist camp would, of course, look on this whole method with a certain shudder of horror. Otto Jespersen is a case in point. He describes a series exercise and says, "I scarcely think that Gouin's ideas ought to be used for more than such occasional series" (Jespersen 1904, 137). This might imply that Jespersen saw some practical merit in the series method, but not in the rationalist theory upon which it was built. That is Jespersen's only comment, except for this note: "I am tempted here to enlarge upon Gouin's method of teaching languages, but I have neither the space, nor exactly the desire, to do so, since I have never seen it carried out in practice. I can refer to R. Kron's (certainly too enthusiastic) description. . . . and to Brekke's (for me absolutely convincing) criticism . . ." (Jespersen 1904, 137-138; cf. Brekke 1894).

The most interesting thing about Jespersen's note is that Brekke hardly gives any serious criticism of Gouin at all, much less an "absolutely convincing criticism." Rather, he gives a straight description of the series method as it was practiced in London. Even when he points out cases of difficulty and failure, he always makes allowances and indicates that they could be remedied within the system. One can only assume that Gouin's notions were so different from Jespersen's, that Jespersen read the mere statement of Gouin's ideas as an exposé of something untenable. Brekke points out that the "subjective language" is badly organized in the series method, but that instruction in it is essential in making the series method work. This is quite a burden on the teacher, and Brekke has hit upon a fundamental weakness of Gouin's method. But otherwise, if one has a competent teacher who can speak the language, who can handle his students, and who can conduct a lively class, then, Brekke says, we have a very acceptable method that will give a good knowledge to the student (pp. 75-76). Of ordering the language in series, Brekke says this is a brilliant or ingenious idea (p. 78). In general, Brekke gives a very straightforward description of the fact that the series method produced excellent results with the able teachers he observed in London. Jespersen's reaction—taking an honest description to be an "absolutely convincing criticism"—only underlines the tremendous difference between the empiricist and rationalist approaches to foreign language teaching.

A comparison between the series method and mim-mem pattern drill is instructive. In spite of a certain superficial similarity, the difference is profound: In the first place, the organization of Gouin's exercises makes them so easy to learn that he does not have to insist on rote memory at all. Several exercises are learned each class hour, and there is no actual need for homework. Second, the changing of tense or person in an exercise is quite unlike a pattern drill in that the student is forced by the nature of the exercise to think about the real phenomenon he is describing. The changes of structure are matters of peripheral attention. To use the phrase of the structuralists, the student is forced to think first about *what* he is saying, and then *how* he says it. This is so because of the way in which the series exercises are so closely bound to the order of things in ordinary experience. In learning a series, the student does not memorize, for example, that one grasps a doorknob before he turns it; this is already known by the student, and it is given by experience. Therefore, in order to repeat the series, he has to visualize the action itself so that he can remember the order of the events he is describing. Otherwise the feat of memory would be impossible.

The advocates of pattern drill give their students much practice in *how* to say things, divorcing this practice from contexts of real content, and paying little attention to what is actually being said. They assume that the students will somehow be able to say things automatically when an appropriate context arrives. Gouin recognized that students actually need a much different kind of practice: they must practice saying things in real contexts where the content of what is said is at least as important as the linguistic structure being manipulated. Only in this way can the student develop a "grammatical sense" in which the rules of the language automatically link the content of speech to its expression. In pattern drills, structures are manipulated as ends in themselves; in Gouin's system, language is always used as a means for the representation of a concept. We do not have "drill" in the series system; we have "meaningful practice."

The real weakness in the series method lies in the fact that Gouin latched on to one experience in the life of a three-year-old and constructed his entire method out of this single episode in the development of language. At that time, the verb is supremely important to the child's learning of language, and likewise, the organization of events in the sequence of time. But Gouin did not observe his nephew in earlier stages of language development when *naming* was important and when the verb hardly existed at all in the child's language. Nor did he observe the development of language through stories which the child heard, or later, which he read for himself. The whole method was based on the experience at the mill, and Gouin constructed 4,000 exercises on this model.

The neglect of naming meant that Gouin had no way of beginning his foreign language instruction without recourse to the student's native language. Brekke tells us that it takes three months of instruction, one hour a day, before the mother tongue can be avoided in the language classroom. Gouin shares this fault with the mim-mem and pattern drill of the empiricists, but our discussion in the next chapter will show that it is nevertheless a fault which can and should be avoided. Gouin's neglect of the way children learn language through stories led him to neglect any reading which was not in series form.

By emphasizing so much the organization of events in sequence of time, Gouin also seems to have overlooked the other ways in which people organize their conceptions. For example, it is well known that the parts of the body and the items of clothing can be learned very quickly in a foreign language when they are organized in their natural spatial relationships. This is a serious oversight.

The unorganized state of Gouin's "subjective language," as we have seen, was another basic weakness in Gouin's method. Like Brekke, de Sauzé feels that Gouin's subjective language is too meager, and that his "figurative language" is too vague (cf. Barall 1949, 45). Perhaps we should make the even stronger criticism that Gouin went wrong in the first place when he set up such a wide gulf between the "subjective language" and the "objective language." Both would seem to be generated by the same set of generative rules, but Gouin seems almost to treat the sentences of the subjective language as if they were separate elements of language which must be learned individually.

Gouin had one brilliant insight into language learning, and he carried this idea so long and far that he ended up with a very rigid method for teaching languages. Yet it was a fertile insight, with many corollaries, and the depth of Gouin's one insight gave him an understanding of language learning that is rarely equaled among language teachers.

CHAPTER 7

THE DIRECT METHOD OF BERLITZ AND DE SAUZÉ

The "direct method," properly speaking, refers most appropriately to language teaching methods like those of Berlitz and de Sauzé in which the mother tongue is excluded both from the classroom and from the textbook, and in which communication is built up in a step by step progression through a question and answer dialog between the teacher and the student.

This is basically a "common-sense" method, given rationalist presuppositions about language learning, and it has been invented over and over again throughout the years, sometimes with various other names.[16] Berlitz and de Sauzé provide the best and most sophisticated examples of this method and its rationale, but they have no particular claims of originality in inventing the method.

[16] Heness (1875) and Sauveur (1875) had what they called "natural methods"; Gourio (1921) called his the "direct method"; de Sauzé (1929) used the terms "Cleveland Plan" and "Multiple Approach"; Berlitz (1887) called it the "Berlitz Method"; Lénard (1965), the "Verbal-Active Method."

Common-sense method though it may be, skepticism is frequently voiced by those who have never seen it in operation or by those who do not share the rationalist presuppositions about language learning. "It would never work to exclude the mother tongue in teaching a noncognate language like Japanese," they say, "or for English in Japan." But quite on the contrary, the Berlitz schools seem to have little trouble excluding the mother tongue with Japanese in America or with English in Japan. The skepticism is usually due to a lack of understanding—in most cases it is accompanied by some such misconception as that the teacher just starts jabbering away in his language and lets the students catch on as soon as they can. That, of course, is not a sensible way to teach a language. Exclusion of the mother tongue from the language classroom cannot work unless it is accompanied by the proper ordering of vocabulary and grammatical points in order to provide a step by step progression.

Exclusive use of the foreign language in the classroom is the most distinctive and perhaps the most important feature of the direct method. But a convincing case cannot be made for it without the other features that make it possible. So let us turn to the principles of the direct method, saving till last our discussion of the exclusive use of the foreign language.

1. Step by step progression

To establish communication with someone who doesn't know our language, we must start with small beginnings and then build from there. We start with naming, as the infant does, pointing to things and giving them names. This simple act of communication is a delight to the child learning his first language, and this same delight comes to the person learning a second language when he realizes that he can communicate in a language that he didn't know an hour before.

In the first lesson of English, Berlitz (1967) teaches sixteen nouns: *pencil, pen, book, box, paper, key, chair, table, lamp, door, window, telephone, wall, ceiling, floor, room*. He teaches the question, "What is this?", and the answer, "It is a pencil." There are two other questions in the first lesson: "Is this a pencil?" (with the answers, "Yes, it is a pencil," and "No, it is not a pencil."), and "Is this a pencil or a pen?" (with the answer, "It is a pen."). Besides this, he teaches the numbers one through five. Altogether there are thirty words: the sixteen nouns listed above, and *is, what, a, or, not, yes, no, this, it, one, two, three, four, five*. All this can be taught in forty-five minutes without recourse to the student's native language.

At this level of language learning it does not help much to have a cognate language. Only a half dozen of these thirty words are obviously cognate (to the uninitiated) with either French or with German. The meaning of these words and the grammatical constructions is taught by their use in the pattern of communication.

The important things of lesson one are 1) naming, and 2) the questions and answers which go along with naming. The particular nouns to teach depend on the interests of the student and teacher, and upon what is available to point to. De Sauzé teaches such greetings as "Bonjour" right away, which is nice, but nothing seems to be hurt by waiting till the second and third lesson for this sort of expression as Berlitz does. De Sauzé also contrasts *this* and *that* in the first lesson, which is good in helping to distinguish *this* from *it*, but Berlitz waits until lesson six to introduce *that*. A certain amount of discretion is allowable for this sort of thing. And with different languages you have different grammatical problems to worry about. In French, for example, de Sauzé introduces masculine and feminine gender in the first lesson.

We have made it through the first lesson with only one verb, *is*, and it appeared only in the third person singular with neuter subjects. Berlitz finds that this one form will do for three more lessons, before he finally introduces *am* and *are*.

Lesson two for Berlitz is largely a repeat of lesson one, with emphasis on the names for clothes (eighteen nouns). He also teaches the numbers six through ten, and the expressions "Good morning. How are you? Fine, thank you. And you?" Thirty new words are learned, with practice in making the previous lesson's grammar automatic. Half of the words from lesson one are required for the questions and answers. There is also time enough to review the sixteen nouns of the previous lesson as well.

Lesson three introduces adjectives by teaching the words for colors. Things learned before are all reviewed by asking what color they are. Lesson four, "Dimensions," gives practice on both predicate adjectives and attributive adjectives through such statements as "The black pencil is long" (elicited by asking, "Is the black pencil long or short?"). Already we see how we build on previous lessons and review them at the same time; once we know a few nouns, adjectives are easy.

In the first four lessons, the student has learned about 120 words, mostly nouns and adjectives. At this point, in the fifth lesson, Berlitz finally gets to *I am, you are, he is,* and *she is,* in a lesson on "Who is this?" It shows remarkable restraint to wait for lesson five before introducing any verb forms besides the neuter of the third person singular, *it is.* But it is precisely this kind of restraint that allows the direct method to work. First things must come first. And even now he still delays in introducing the plural forms.

The sixth lesson brings the plural of verbs and the plural personal pronouns. Besides *to be*, we have the verbs *open* and *close*, which are introduced by opening and closing books. The numbers, which have been introduced five or so at a lesson, finally get to *one hundred, one thousand, one hundred thousand,* and *one million.* And in the process of learning this, we even get the possessive adjectives and possessive pronouns (*my, mine,* etc.). In six lessons we have already gotten to rather complicated matters: the student's grammatical apparatus is ready to blossom.

The seventh lesson brings the present progressive form of the verb ("I am standing; you are sitting"), as well as such words as *on, under, behind, in front of*.

The trend is obvious by now. Thirty words a lesson are learned, and the grammar is built up slowly but surely, one point at a time. By Lesson 26 we are ready for the past tense of verbs ("What did we do yesterday?"); Lesson 27 brings "What have we done before now?" with the present perfect tense; and in Lesson 28 we get the future ("What will happen tomorrow?"). By Lesson 30 we have progressed to the point where we can discuss "Man and his emotions," explaining such abstract concepts as *love, anger,* and *fear.*

After thirty-seven lessons, we will have finished the Berlitz *English: First Book*, and the student will have a good knowledge of basic conversational English. How long will it take to get through these thirty-seven lessons? With a tutor in a Berlitz School it will take roughly seventy-four to one -hundred-and-twenty hours of instruction, depending on the language aptitude of the student. With the Berlitz technique of "total immersion"—eleven forty-five minute sessions a day with a tutor—the average student of high motivation can master this in about two weeks.[17] These figures presuppose very little homework, although Berlitz is now beginning to introduce home review tapes on cassettes. De Sauzé would take it slower in high schools where he would not want to leave anyone behind. He would spend five classes on each lesson (not assigning any homework), and would take thirty-six weeks (a whole school year) to cover this much material.[18]

At this point the student will be able to use actively all of the basic grammatical apparatus of English, and he will have a vocabulary of about 1100 words. This is enough to "get along" in English, to conduct intelligent conversations, to travel and go shopping. This basic vocabulary will account for about 70 per cent of the words we see on the average written page. But it is still a far cry from the 50,000 word vocabulary of the seven-year-old native speaker, or the 150,000 of the teenager, or the 200,000 plus of the adult. The student will still be unable to understand very much on radio or T.V.

With step by step progression, putting emphasis on one simple grammatical point at a time, we can see that it is quite

[17] I wish to thank Dr. Gerhard Stieglitz, Vice-President for Research of the Berlitz Schools, for providing these estimates and for checking other facts in this chapter. He is not, of course, to blame for the fact that I depart from the Berlitz Method in favor of other versions of the Direct Method, particularly in how to teach reading and writing and in the necessity to study grammar consciously. Two fully orthodox descriptions of the Berlitz Method can be found in the prefaces to the early Berlitz textbooks (e.g., Berlitz (1887) and in Stieglitz (1955).

[18] These calculations do not take account of the fact that speakers of languages related to English (e.g., German) will learn English faster than will speakers of unrelated languages (e.g., Japanese). These other variables are discussed in chapter nine.

possible to teach a foreign language without ever using the student's native tongue. Once we have finished the elementary lessons, we have reached the point where step by step progression of this type can be abandoned, and the language can be used easily in the intermediate and advanced classes. But bilingualism is still a long way off, and systematic study of some sort must continue if progress is to be made in the foreign language.

2. Paraphrase

Granted, now, that it is possible to exclude the student's mother tongue from the classroom, through adequate organization and step by step progression, won't it still be the case, the skeptic asks, that it will save a lot of time and effort to lapse into the mother tongue to explain things every now and then?

Perhaps you will save time and effort in the short run by using the student's native tongue occasionally. But in the long run, you lose time. To get a person to think in a foreign language and to use it for communication, we must provide him with something serious to think about. We must provide something challenging. Simple drills are dull if there is no possibility for error. But there is nothing more challenging in a foreign language than trying to learn something new while using the language. If the teacher reverts to the student's native language every time he has something serious to say, then he loses his best opportunities to get the student to concentrate and to think in the foreign language.

To explain new things in a foreign language, you use the technique of "paraphrase." De Sauzé provides the following example of how to explain the word *glace*. He could say "*glace* means 'ice,' " or he could point to a picture of a piece of ice. But he prefers this paraphrase: "En été l'eau du lac est liquide; en hiver l'eau du lac n'est pas liquide, elle est solide; l'eau solide est de la glace" (In summer, the water in a lake is liquid. In winter the water in a lake is not liquid; it is solid. Solid water is ice.). Then he asks questions to make sure they understand the concept and to give them practice in using the word: "En quelle saison y a-t-il de la glace? Y a-t-il de la glace au printemps? en été? en hiver? Y a-t-il de la glace maintenant? Fait-il chaud, quand il y a de la glace sur le lac?" (In what season do we have ice? Is there ice in springtime? In summer? In winter? Is there any ice now? Is it cold when there is ice on the lake?) (de Sauzé 1929, 16). Thus the student practices what he already knows of the foreign language while he concentrates on the serious business of learning something new about the language.

The law of "incubation" (which we discussed in the chapter on Gouin) states that there is a certain time lag before a short-term memory becomes a long-term memory, and that during this time it is important to reinforce the memory to make sure it is not forgotten. The technique of paraphrase is ideal for practicing and reinforcing the memory of previously learned words while using them to learn new words and constructions. In addition, the student will never have to stop when he sees this new word again, and translate the word to his native language in order to remember the meaning.

3. Grammar in the Direct Method

The crucial role of grammar in the direct method is obvious from the way the lessons are organized to build up the knowledge of grammar in a step-by-step progression.

Students are not told the rule, however, before they see examples of it in operation and are allowed to figure the rule out for themselves. "Instead of presenting the student with a rule on a platter," as de Sauzé says, "We set up a few carefully chosen illustrations of that rule and we lead him to discover through skillful guidance the relationship of the new element to others previously mastered and to formulate his observations into a law governing those cases" (de Sauzé 1929, 14).

Berlitz is satisfied if the student just figures out what is going on and then generates his own sentences using the new rule without actually formulating what he has learned. But de Sauzé was probably right in putting more emphasis on conscious reasoning. As we have already quoted him as saying, "We found . . . in our experiment that the practical results, such as reading, writing, speaking, and understanding, were achieved in greater proportion and in less time when the technique involved a maximum amount of conscious reasoning" (de Sauzé 1953, 5). He told his teachers to "insist upon a scientific attitude on the part of your students toward language; reason, analyze the forms used, even the spelling of sounds, by frequently asking *pourquoi* [why]" (de Sauzé 1929, 48).

De Sauzé carries grammar study well beyond the elementary stages of language learning. For French, the irregular verbs are studied with verb charts (de Sauzé 1922) during the third semester of the high school curriculum. After that, students spend one day a week studying *Grammaire Française* (de Sauzé and True 1920), a more or less traditional reference grammar with numerous exercises, written entirely in French.

If a mistake is made, de Sauzé does not correct the student directly. If the student has pronounced a silent final -*e*, for example, de Sauzé would ask whether the final -*e* was pronounced or silent. The student would then reason out the proper pronunciation and would correct himself. This is a very effective way in getting the student to avoid that mistake again—much more effective than merely having the student mimic the correct form without thinking. If a student makes a mistake in gender, de Sauzé would ask whether that given word is masculine or feminine. If there is a mistake in word order, de Sauzé would ask why the student used that particular word order. Notice how different this attitude toward mistakes is from the fear which the empiricists have of the mistake which they think is the beginning of a bad habit. De Sauzé knows that mistakes are easily eradicated once the student understands what is wrong. Conscious reasoning also helps to avoid mistakes by developing the student's grammatical intuition and by giving him a basis for applying the rules to new cases: it will "multiply his experience a thousand times (de Sauzé 1929, 4).

4. Writing and reading

Writing is usually taught from the first day with the direct method, thus reinforcing the memory of each new word and expression with an additional mode of perception.

For de Sauzé, in the first year of a beginning high school course, virtually everything a student says he also writes on the blackboard. Suppose, for example, that there is a book on the teacher's desk. He would ask the first student, "Where is the book?" The student answers, "The book is on the desk." "Write it on the blackboard," the teacher would say, then he would proceed to the second student while the first one was going to the blackboard. "Is the book on the table?" "No, the book isn't on the table." Then the second student would go to the blackboard to write his answer. After the students have all been asked a question, and the board is full of their answers, the whole class goes over the sentences at the blackboard and corrects them.

At every point in the course, the students can write everything that they can say. If they are able to speak it and write it, they can read it. For a long time the student's reading is limited primarily to what is written on the blackboard. The textbook is ignored in class, and is useful only to help the student review his lesson at home. Bright students have been known to go through six weeks of class without opening their textbook and without even realizing that the teacher was following the textbook.

De Sauzé was convinced that the simultaneous learning of listening, speaking, writing, and reading is very important in language learning. But particularly it is the productive aspects of language—speaking and writing—that are essential in mastering the receptive aspects of listening and reading. A student cannot have a clear idea of a sentence he hears or reads unless it is a sentence for which he has the grammatical competence which underlies its production. When a person "understands" something which is beyond his capacity to produce, guesswork is involved. De Sauze would not tolerate "vagueness and 'à peu près' " in a student's understanding of the reading (1929, 91). If a student wants real reading power, he must have active control over what he reads. It is for this reason that de Sauzé maintained that the only effective way to attain the goal of a "reading knowledge" of a language is to gain an active mastery of the productive aspects of that language.

5. Interest

For de Sauzé, "the most vital problem in any classroom is how to stimulate and retain the interest of the pupils" (de Sauzé 1929, 8). Few teachers would deny that the interest of the pupils is important, but for de Sauzé this point receives extraordinary emphasis—it is the first of the fundamental principles he discusses in his teachers' manual. He quotes Anatole France as saying that "The art of teaching is only the art of interesting, of arousing curiosity, and curiosity is active only in happy minds" (de Sauzé 1929, 8).

Everything in de Sauzé's methodology is subservient to the principle of interest. The method itself must be inherently interesting. One should not depend on the personality of the teacher or variety of technique to arouse curiosity and motivation in the student. De Sauzé remarks that "the little girl who once told her teacher, 'Now what are you going to amuse us with today,' was perfectly conscious and pointedly critical of that type of teaching supposedly interesting" (de Sauzé 1929, 8). Instead of "amusing" the students, the good teacher challenges them: he forces them to use the foreign language for genuine communication from the very first day of class, carefully grading the difficulties so that the student can accomplish the task set before him. A method which is inherently interesting to the student is also interesting to the teacher. If one insists on meaningful practice rather than drill, then the teacher as well as the student is engaged in meaningful activity. The teacher is not merely a drillmaster or a person who hears recitations. On the contrary, he is actively involved in the student's learning process.

CHAPTER 8

A DIGRESSION CONCERNING TWO "HERESIES"

In recent years there has been an increasing amount of criticism of the empiricist theory of language learning and its associated methods of language teaching, mim-mem and pattern drill. Some critics, such as Saporta (1964), and Jakobovits (1970), have been at a loss to suggest viable alternatives to the teaching methods. Jakobovits, for example, encourages the teacher to be pragmatic and eclectic in choosing his methods, saying that "Practitioners, such as teachers and therapists, need not feel that they must take sides in theoretical controversies and should desist from their attempts to justify their practices by appealing to particular theories" (Jakobovits 1970, 120).

But besides the skeptical criticisms, there are two opposing suggestions about how language teaching should be changed in light of Chomsky's transformational generative grammar. I will call them "Heresy I" and "Heresy II." The first is that a transformational generative grammar should be drilled into the student using techniques of mim-mem and pattern drill; the second, that the rationalist theory of language learning implies either that a) we should abandon formal instruction altogether, or at least that b) we should avoid instruction in grammar and abandon the use of materials that are ordered according to grammatical difficulty.

I assume that "heresy" is a friendly word to those who hold these positions, since the people I quote probably do not mind being iconoclastic. Yet both positions are at odds with the rationalist theory of language learning and with what I consider to be good language teaching methodology. Let us examine each "heresy" in detail.

1. Heresy   I: that transformational generative grammar should be drilled into the student using the methods of mim-mem and pattern drill

When transformational grammar began to catch on in the early 1960's, the first reaction of many applied linguists was to think that the transformation drill component should be increased, but that otherwise the language teaching business should continue as usual with mim-mem and pattern drill. William Moulton had predicted this reaction in his review article on *Linguistics and Language Teaching in the United States, 1940-1960* (Moulton 1961). He asked how the teacher would react to transformational grammar, and then made what may have been a self-fulfilling prophecy: "Though transformation grammar is too new to permit predictions, it seems likely that it can have far reaching effects in improving both the presentation of grammatical structure in textbooks and the learning of grammatical structure through classroom drill" (Moulton 1961, 108). As we have mentioned, some linguists, like Sol Saporta (1964), were concerned by the fact that Chomsky's rationalist linguistic theory had undermined the basis for mim-mem and pattern drill, for it seemed clear in light of Chomsky's theories that mim-mem and pattern drill were misconceived methods of teaching a language. But this point did not bother those who adopted our "Heresy   I." David DeCamp, for example, in his chapter on *Linguistics and Teaching Foreign Languages* (1969), acknowledges that Chomsky's theories have superceded Leonard Bloomfield's behaviorism. But he maintains in spite of this that "The best modern language courses still must include a great deal of mimicry and memorization. There is no substitute for them in language learning" (p. 142). And "The core of all good language teaching is still active pattern drill. It is just that we now try harder to make the student aware of what is happening during the pattern drill, to enlist his active cooperation, and to take advantage of his human ability to do what Pavlov's dog could not do." (p. 143). DeCamp then goes on to reiterate what is involved in the methods of mim-mem and pattern drill, using Twaddell's terminology for the five stages of (1) recognition, (2) imitation, (3) repetition, (4) variation, and (5) selection (see chapter five, above). Nothing much seems changed.

The essence of the argument against "Heresy I" is indicated in Bernard Spolsky's paper *Linguistics and Language Pedagogy: Applications or Implications* (1969). One simply has to distinguish between the *applications* of linguistics and its *implications*, and sometimes there will be implications which rule out certain applications.

Applications of linguistics can be made where they are not justified. The people of Heresy I are trying to apply transformational grammar within the framework of their behaviorist-based methods of language teaching. But the *implications* of Chomsky's theories are that the behavioristic reasons for using mim-mem and pattern drill are no longer valid. If we rule out these teaching methods, the question of using transformational grammar in these methods can no longer arise.

Leonard Newmark points out the "temptations" of this heresy in his paper *Grammatical Theory and the Teaching of English as a Foreign Language* (Newmark 1963). He lists a number of these temptations which transformational grammar presents to the textbook writer: it provides the most elegant grammatical descriptions; it has ordered rules which might provide order for the textbook; transformation drills are easy to use, and so on. But he then goes on to argue that "these appeals are deceptive, all wrong, for the language teacher" (Newmark 1963, 217).

William Rutherford succumbed to these temptations, however, in writing *Modern English* (1968), a textbook for foreign students. He proclaims that "The linguistic orientation of the work is that of *generative* or *transformational grammar*" (p. ix), and he tries to make applications of the technical parts of transformational grammar in writing his drills. But he doesn't take seriously the pedagogical implications of Chomsky's theories—"transformational theory as such does not tell us exactly how languages are learned" (p. ix)—so except for the transformational terminology, the result is a book which looks very much like any other textbook using the methods of mimicry, memorization, and pattern drill.

Chomsky himself seems to believe that the implications of rationalist theory are much more important to language teaching than are applications of transformational grammar. In talking on linguistic theory at the Northeast Conference on the Teaching of Foreign Language (Chomsky 1966b), he did not mention such words as "phrase structure rules" and "transformation." One of the implications of the theory of generative grammar is that certain mechanical devices for describing languages probably should not be applied to language textbooks. There is, after all, no reason why technical devices which are necessary for descriptive adequacy will also be necessary or even helpful for learning the language. That is why it makes little difference that Gouin, Berlitz, and de Sauzé did not know about transformational grammar; they understood the implications of rationalist theory and constructed methods which are remarkably relevant to our present situation.

2. Heresy II: that the rationalist theory of language learning implies either that a) we should abandon formal instruction altogether, or at least that b) we should avoid instruction in grammar and abandon the use of materials that are ordered according to grammatical difficulty

It is unfortunate that the two best critics of the first heresy manage to go all the way over to the other extreme to propose the second heresy.

Spolsky has made the most radical suggestions. In a paper titled *The Value of Volunteers in English Language Teaching, Or Why Pay For It When You Can Get It For Nothing* (1968), he proposes that we consider abandoning formal instruction altogether, leaving language learning to the combination of a volunteer student with a volunteer teacher.

In an earlier article, Spolsky expresses a profound pessimism about the art of language teaching by saying: "Because we don't know how to teach foreign languages, we grab at any new technique in the hope that it might be the magic key to unlock the gift of tongues" (Spolsky 1966, 119). That statement certainly does not apply to those teachers in the Berlitz and de Sauzé tradition who *do* know a great deal about language teaching.

Newmark and Reibel (1968; see also Newmark 1966, 1967 and Reibel 1969) argue that there have been others who also knew a great deal about language teaching: namely, the linguists (including Newmark) who wrote the Spoken Languages series for the Army during World War II. They call for a return to the mim-mem of those army manuals.

Spolsky, Newmark, and Reibel are all anti-behaviorists and all claim allegiance to the rationalist theory of language learning. But it is a heretical version of the rationalist theory on which they base their suggestions either to abandon formal instruction altogether (Spolsky) or to avoid instruction in grammar and to abandon the use of materials which are graded according to grammatical difficulty (Newmark and Reibel).

The basic premise of this position is that the systematic study of grammar is neither necessary nor sufficient for language learning. This premise may literally be true, but it is highly misleading. Newmark and Reibel's argument goes like this: 1) the study of grammar is not necessary for children and it is not sufficient for adults; 2) meaningful exposure is sufficient for children and necessary for adults; 3) therefore, the study of grammar is neither necessary nor sufficient, and meaningful exposure is both necessary and sufficient. Now the trouble is that the necessity and the sufficiency are attributed to children in the one case and to adults in the other. The argument falls flat unless children and adults learn languages in exactly the same way. Otherwise, the question is still open as to whether meaningful exposure is sufficient for adults.

The facts would indicate that meaningful exposure may be sufficient for some adults, but not for all. Newmark and

Reibel (1968) seem to have observed this fact when they state that it is not motivation which makes the difference: "there are cases galore of immigrants whose very livelihood depends on their mastering a language which nevertheless largely eludes them, and not a few cases of good language learners whose general reward will be no greater than one more A in a language course" (Newmark and Reibel 1968).

Newmark and Reibel are right in insisting that adults can learn languages; they are wrong in assuming that adults and children learn languages basically in the same way, and in asserting that the only differences between the ways adults and children learn languages are quantitative rather than qualitative. In fact they are doubly wrong when they say that adults are quantitatively worse (because of their inferior pronunciation). As we argued above in Chapter 3 section 3, adults are clearly superior to children in language learning except for pronunciation; and part of the adult's superiority stems from the fact that he can reason grammatically. The ability to reason grammatically versus the lack of this ability is a *qualitative* difference between adults and children. Likewise the ability to acquire perfect pronunciation versus the lack of this ability is probably a qualitative difference.

Children and adults are different. And while meaningful exposure may be sufficient for some adults, it is much more *efficient* for most adults if there can be meaningful practice of the grammatical constructions of the language in an orderly way. Attention to grammar can be extremely helpful to adults in the context of meaningful practice. When adults are well taught, they can learn languages much faster than children can, whereas the child's only real advantage is pronunciation (see above, Chapter 3 section 3).

At one point in their article, Newmark and Reibel give unwitting evidence that the study of grammar might be a beneficial adjunct to meaningful exposure. They quote Bandura and Walters *Social Learning and Personality Development* (1965, 106) for support that behavior can be acquired just by watching a demonstration of this behavior, without behavioristic drill and reinforcement. They over-looked one phrase in the quote: "Following demonstrations by a model, *or* (though to a lesser extent) *following verbal descriptions of desired behavior* (emphasis added), the learner gradually reproduces more or less the entire response pattern, even though he may perform no overt response, and consequently receive no reinforcement, throughout the demonstration period." (quoted in Newmark and Reibel 1968, 236.) In language study the analogue to "following verbal descriptions of desired behavior" is presumably the conscious study of grammar.

Now, surely such grammar study is not terribly effective by itself, without meaningful use of the language. Gouin's memorization of the German grammar, roots, and dictionary, as we saw in chapter six above, was a *reductio ad absurdum* of this kind of isolated study. But that does *not* imply that grammar study should be abandoned! If oxygen is not sufficient to fight a fire with, you should not therefore abandon the use of all compounds which contain oxygen (like H_2O, for example). Conscious attention to grammar in the context of meaningful use and meaningful practice (as in de Sauzé's direct method) is an extremely powerful combination for adult foreign language learning.

In spite of the fact that Newmark and Reibel have rejected Bloomfield's behaviorism, they call for a return to the language teaching methods which Bloomfield himself used, the memorization of dialogs and the use of canned conversations based on these dialogs. Here is a question and answer from Newmark and Reibel: "How can the evident success of the child's language learning method be realized for foreign language teaching to adults? The proponents of the various 'direct methods' have developed numerous techniques that attempt to do this; and linguists have done even better than the more physicalistic of the direct methodists, by utilizing the powerful tool of dialogue memorization, which at its best provides less limiting and more realistic contexts for learning than can be provided if the strictures (e.g., no translation, structurally limited lessons) of the more rigid of the direct methodists are adhered to" (Newmark and Reibel 1968, 238-239).

But how is dialog memorization like the child's method of language learning? If there is one thing the child does not do, and cannot do, it is to memorize dialogs. In addition, this is one of the universally disliked features of junior high and high school foreign language classes.

Why settle for "realistic" contexts when with the direct method you can have *real* contexts for language use? Memorization of dialogs is a highly artificial method of language teaching, and the conversations based on these dialogs are no less artificial (the examples given by Newmark and Reibel are only one step better than translation exercises).[19]

Newmark and Reibel state that "The pedagogical implication of our position is that we abandon the notion of structural grading and structural ordering" (Newmark and Reibel 1968, 239). But if there is a second thing which the child does not do, it is to avoid structural grading and structural ordering (i.e., grading according to grammatical difficulty). The first utterances of a child are things like "Hi!" and "Cracker." After a while the child begins using three-word utterances, and it is a long time before he uses sentences which are grammatically complicated.

The only reasons which Newmark and Reibel use to justify

[19] In these examples from Newmark and Reibel, the Students are told in English exactly what is to be said in French. But in addition to translation, the student has to change the sentences from indirect discourse (English) to direct discourse (French). Here is one of the examples of a conversation to be given in French:

"Conversation 1
 You are on the bus with a friend and spot Jules to whom you owe some money. Your friend is about to call over to Jules.
You. . . Tell your friend to pretend that he is looking out of the window.
He. . . . Asks you why, he's about to call over to Jules.
You. . . Tell him that Jules is looking for you, that you owe him money.
He. . . . Says O.K., but not to worry, Jules has probably not noticed you." (Newmark and Reibel 1968, 252).

the abandonment of grammatical ordering are that children and adults are the same, and that children manage pretty well with grammatically unordered materials. We have argued that children and adults are different. But even if Newmark and Reibel were right on these propositions, it would not follow that we should therefore exclude grammatically ordered materials from the adult foreign language classroom. The child faces a tremendous task in imposing order on the language materials he is exposed to. The grammar of a language does not suddenly pop into a child's head after 300 or even 1000 hours of exposure to the language—not even 300 or 1000 hours after he says his first sentence. Studies on the acquisition of syntax in children are quite clear in showing the gradual development of grammar over a period of several years (see for example, Carol Chomsky 1969). Yet after 300 hours of instruction using grammatically ordered materials in meaningful contexts, an adult can gain a fluent conversational knowledge of a language, and after 1000 hours he can be quite proficient—worthy of the term *bilingual* (see below, chapter eleven).

It is pedagogically irresponsible to give up powerful teaching devices (or to give up teaching altogether), just because children learn the basics of their native language before they enter school. The rationalist theory of language learning does not imply that we should be irresponsible teachers.

PART IV

CONCLUSIONS

CHAPTER 9

RESEARCH STUDIES ON THE EFFECTIVENESS
OF VARIOUS METHODS

It is an undeniable fact that some methods of language teaching are more effective than other methods. Any person who has studied a half dozen languages under widely differing methods will testify to that fact. Consider, for example, my own experiences. I spent a fourth of my time for a whole academic year (360 hours, 120 of it in class) to gain a passive knowledge of classical Greek grammar and a basic vocabulary of 1,000 words. I was unable to speak, write, or think in Greek, but I could decode it and translate. The next summer I spent eight days studying Portuguese before a trip to Brazil (80 hours, 15 of it with a tutor using the direct method). In that short time I gained active control of the basic grammar of Portuguese and a vocabulary of 1,500 words. I was able to speak, write, and think in Portuguese within the limits of my vocabulary. That was enough for travel and shopping in Brazil; and soon after I arrived there I had a four-hour conversation with a law student without running out of things to say. I am certain that there is a world of difference between teaching methods. My experience with mimicry-memorization came later, when I studied Mandarin Chinese as a graduate student. The results were almost the same as with Greek. After studying Chinese

for 360 hours I had a passive knowledge of its elementary
vocabulary and grammar. I could take dictation and translate,
but I couldn't think in the language or say new things. With
mim-mem, however, I did gain a near-native pronunciation of
Chinese.

Why was I able to gain an active knowledge of elementary
Portuguese four times as fast as I could get a passive
knowledge of Greek or Chinese? Unfortunately there are
other factors besides teaching method which help explain my
success with Portuguese: Portuguese has many similarities to
English, and even more to French (which I had studied for
two and a half years). And with Portuguese I had a tutor,
whereas I was in ordinary classes for Greek and Chinese. The
intensiveness of my Portuguese study may also have helped.
But even if these factors could account for the 4 to 1
difference in my speed of learning, they could hardly account
for the fact that with Greek and Chinese I had a purely
passive knowledge, whereas with Portuguese I had an active
knowledge and could think without translating.

My experiences with first-year French and German corrob-
orate the opinion that the teaching method makes the
difference between an active and a passive knowledge of a
language. In both cases I learned similar amounts of
vocabulary and grammar, but with French (direct method) I
had an active knowledge of the language, and with German
(reading method) I had only a passive knowledge.

It can be said, of course, that my own experiences are
nothing more than hearsay, anecdotal evidence. They are
convincing only to me. If they have general validity, one
might expect that educational researchers would have proved
the superiority of the direct method with their statistical
analysis. Unfortunately, educational research hasn't been able
to prove much of anything about language learning. After
reviewing the research on foreign-language teaching, John B.
Carroll pointed out that "Educational research has contributed very little to foreign language teaching aside from general
knowledge concerning the construction of achievement tests,
the role of foreign language aptitude in the learning process,
and the psychology of bilingualism" (Carroll 1963a, 1094;
see also Carroll 1966a and 1969).

It is evident that an astute critic can find technical flaws—or even worse, serious conceptual errors—in almost every research study of foreign language teaching. At best we get some "unassailable facts that . . . will not be news to anyone" such as that "students vary widely in the levels of mastery that they attain in one or two years of high school foreign-language instruction" (Carroll 1969, 233). More normally the studies are suggestive but not conclusive. And then there is no lack of totally ill-conceived research studies.

The biggest technical difficulty with research on language teaching is that there are so many variables to deal with. We have seen that problem already in the discussion of how my experience with Portuguese differed from my experience with Greek.

The most important variables are the *language learning aptitude of the student and the relative difficulty of the foreign language involved.* Language-learning aptitude varies greatly. People with high aptitude can learn language twice as fast as the ordinary person and three times as fast as the low aptitude person. Carroll and Sapon have found that language aptitude is not well correlated to tests of verbal intelligence, but that it is correlated to four other factors which they test in their Modern Language Aptitude Test (Carroll and Sapon 1959). The relative difficulty of various languages depends mainly on how similar the language is to the student's native language (or to other languages he knows). The difficulty of the writing system is also an important consideration to the normal adult who wants to be literate in the foreign language. The Foreign Service Institute groups its languages into four groups of difficulty for native speakers of English. The most difficult languages (e.g., Japanese) require about four months of study to accomplish what can be learned in the easiest languages (e.g., German) in about one month. Russian and Hebrew would fall into intermediate categories, and would require two or three months (Wilds 1962).

Other troublesome variables are the students' and the teachers' attitudes, the student-teacher relationship, class size, number of class hours a week, amount of homework, the age of the students, the students' background with other foreign languages (especially with related languages), the homogeneity of the class, the physical setting, and so on, not to speak of language laboratories and the textbooks and methods used. It is extremely difficult to control all these variables. Different teachers will have radically different classes even when they are using the same textbook and, supposedly, the same method.

Furthermore, there are moral problems with educational experiments. Most conscientious teachers have a certain moral revulsion against teaching in some "pure" but inadequate method just to prove to an experimenter that it is inadequate; they have a responsibility to the student, and they will adjust the given method to their own liking in order to preserve their self-respect. A case in point is the "Pennsylvania Project" which attempted to compare three methods of language teaching: the "traditional method," the "functional skills method," and the "functional skills method with supplementary grammatical explanations" (see Smith 1970 and Carroll 1969). To the surprise of the experimenters, the "traditional method" won. The teachers using the traditional method had been allowed to use the language for oral practice up to 25 per cent of the time—making it already quite different from the grammar-translation method that used to be so prevalent. But apparently the teachers went beyond the 25 per cent in order to preserve their self-respect, and were actually using a method which was halfway between the old grammar-translation method and a very respectable direct method.

The technical details and moral problems of experimentation are not as serious, however, as the conceptual problems. In the case of the Pennsylvania Project, three *methods* of teaching and three *techniques* of language laboratory use were compared without really thinking through whether there was any valid theoretical reason why these methods and techniques should differ from each other. The functional skills method and the functional skills method with grammar both used the same mim-mem and pattern drill textbooks. The grammatical descriptions were in the textbooks whether or not the teacher chose to cover them in class. In both cases the basic methodology of mim-mem and pattern drill was the same, and the added grammatical explanation did not bring with it an attempt to make grammar psychologically real through meaningful practice as the direct method would. Little wonder that the functional skills method and the functional skills method with grammar showed no significant differences in effectiveness. The three language laboratory systems which the Pennsylvania Project compared were also all the same in practical result. And why, indeed, shouldn't they have been the same? The materials used were the same; only the machines were different. One lab had simple tape recorders; the second had audio-active earphones for the tape recorders; the third allowed the student to record himself. Anyone who has used these three systems himself should have realized that there is no significant difference between them if the materials remain the same. I myself even prefer the simple tape recorder in the privacy of my home to the sophisticated but distracting language laboratory.

The trouble with so much educational research is that it has not been used to test any interesting theoretical questions. As Chomsky has put it, "The social and behavioral sciences provide ample evidence that objectivity can be pursued with little consequent gain in insight and understanding. On the other hand, a good case can be made for the view that the natural sciences have, by and large, sought objectivity primarily insofar as it is a tool for gaining insight (for providing phenomena that can suggest or test deeper explanatory hypotheses)." Chomsky sees the true scientist as "one whose concern is for insight and understanding (rather than for objectivity as a goal in itself)" (Chomsky 1965, 20). This description fits de Sauzé perfectly. In describing his experiments with language teaching at Cleveland, de Sauze remarks that

The results secured in those experiments are not available in terms of statistical percentages; we had to content ourselves in many instances with the evidence when accepted as conclusive by the unanimous judgment of all teachers engaged in the experiment, this evidence based mainly upon comparison of present results with those of previous years. Our principal measuring tool was, and still

is, common sense, a tool now in disuse, even in disrepute
in the wave of pseudo-scientific methods which is sweep-
ing over some of our pedagogical institutions (de Sauzé
1929, 3).

If we are going to be serious about understanding the
process of foreign-language learning and teaching, we will
have to go beyond gross statistical measures to make a
number of detailed case studies. Statistics are very useful in
showing, for example, that on the average the students who
major in foreign languages in American colleges have only a
mediocre knowledge of the language they have studied.
Further, statistical methods have shown that on the average
the student who studies abroad has a much greater competence in his foreign language than does the language major
who stays home (cf. Carroll 1967). But then one asks,
"Why?", and the measurements do not help. Carroll has
shown that the typical French major in an American college
scores a "44" on the MLA listening proficiency test at the
time of his graduation. This correlates with the Foreign
Service Institute rating of "S-2," "limited working proficiency." We can safely conclude that we must improve our
language teaching. But what must we do to improve? What
does a "44" on the MLA test mean in terms of what we have
not taught our students? Is their vocabulary made up of the
wrong words? or is it too small? Is pronunciation a major
problem in listening comprehension? Do all students who
score "44" have the same problems? Statistical measures
provide very little specific help in diagnosing the state of a
given individual's foreign-language competence. To understand what goes on in an individual's foreign-language
learning, we will have to study these individual cases in detail,
one at a time.

The test of "common sense" must remain the major
criterion for choosing between different methods of language
teaching and for constructing our own method. But our
common sense is colored to a very large degree by our
education and experience. To someone steeped in behaviorist
theory, mim-mem and pattern drill make sense in a way that
they do not after a person has studied generative grammar
and the rationalist theory of language learning. And firsthand

experience with many language-teaching methods is the only thing which can give an adequate basis for evaluating any given method. A partial understanding of linguistic theory combined with narrow experience can lead to absurd results. A widespread mistaken notion, for example, is that transformational generative grammar should lead to an increased number of pattern drills of the transformational type. But such drills are quite out of keeping with the rationalist theory of language learning, and Chomsky was certainly right in failing even to mention such technicalities as phrase structure rules and transformations when speaking on linguistic theory to the Northeast Conference on the Teaching of Foreign Languages (Chomsky 1966b).

Language teaching in some respects is an art. Teaching ability is learned through happy experiences as a student, through observation of demonstration schools like de Sauzé's, and through apprenticeship to master teachers. But in the last analysis each teacher has to create for himself his own method of teaching, based on his understanding of linguistic theory and on his experience.

I have my own opinions about the merits of various methods, based on my own experiences and on the theoretical considerations raised above. I feel that pattern drills can be discarded without any loss if we use a tightly organized direct method. But mim-mem, Gouin's series method, and the direct method all have a valuable place if used in conjunction with the other methods. Let us review briefly the special advantages of these three methods.

CHAPTER 10

THE ADVANTAGES OF THREE METHODS

*1. Overcoming the adult pronunciation block:
the advantage of Mim-Mem*

Adults have an undeservedly bad reputation as language learners because of their usual difficulty with pronunciation. In other respects, adults can learn languages more effectively than children can, but the typical adult develops a very noticeable foreign accent.

Part of the trouble is that adults have an ambivalent attitude about pronunciation: they often seem to want to keep their accent to show the world that they are foreign. As Haugen says, a foreign accent is a person's best passport (Haugen 1965). Furthermore, the foreign accent covers a multitude of other sins; it warns the listener not to be surprised if he finds other mistakes. And if there are no other mistakes, people will notice how well the foreigner speaks their language.

But if a foreigner wants to adopt a new identity and wants to speak like a native, then the techniques of mimicry and memorization are excellent aids for his task of acquiring perfect pronunciation, particularly with stress and intonation.

The direct method produces pretty good results with pronunciation. Stress and intonation are important integral parts of the grammar, and cannot be avoided in teaching the other parts of the grammar. But perfection is elusive because the grammar of a language allows for wide insignificant variation in pronunciation, and the direct method teacher is not likely to insist on perfect imitation once the student gets within the realm of acceptability.

Pronunciation is a skill which can be separated from knowledge of a language. People can acquire excellent pronunciation without understanding any of the words they are pronouncing so well. Perfection of pronunciation skill requires the concentrated practice which is involved in the mimicry-memorization technique. Note, however, that in recommending mim-mem as a *technique* for perfecting pronunciation, I am not recommending it as a *method* for learning the other aspects of a language.

2. Amassing a sufficiently large vocabulary: The advantage of Gouin's Series Method

François Gouin was one of the few language teachers to take seriously the task of teaching his students a foreign vocabulary comparable to what they already knew in their native language.

We have pointed out that American adults often know about half of the words in the Webster's unabridged dictionary—they have a vocabulary of some 225,000 words. Junior high students know about 100,000 words; seven-year-olds, 50,000 words. There is so much repetition and redundancy in the vocabulary that native speakers can learn new words at the rate of 10,000 a year for their first twenty years. If done right, vocabulary acquisition can be the easiest part of learning a foreign language.

Gouin's series method provides an ingenious way to organize the vocabulary systematically. The series provides a natural context in which many new words can easily be taught and easily remembered. The natural organization of the series allows the student to think directly in the foreign language using the new words.

The series method, however, is not appropriate by itself for the first lessons, since the student's mother tongue would have to be used extensively to get the meaning of the series across. Later on, it would be boring if it were used by itself. But any teacher who seriously wants to teach a large vocabulary to his students in a systematic way ought to consider using something like the series method as a part of his teaching.

3. Learning to generate meaningful sentences and to think in the foreign language: The advantage of the direct method

Knowledge of a language will not be terribly useful nor will it be remembered for a very long time unless it is an active knowledge. The goal of the language classroom is to teach the students to think in the foreign language and to generate meaningful and new sentences in it. The direct method has the student start practicing this on the very first day.

By carefully organizing the grammatical difficulties and proceeding through step-by-step progression from obvious matters to more difficult things, the direct method allows us to exclude the mother tongue from the classroom and to begin communicating in the foreign language right away. It gives the student a functional control of grammar. This makes the direct method both the most effective and the most enjoyable way to teach a foreign language at the elementary level.

CHAPTER 11

LANGUAGE TEACHING TO PRODUCE BILINGUALS

How long does it take to learn a language, to become bilingual? Gouin's calculation is 800 hours—900 for good measure. This would bring a person to the fifteen-year-old language level of a native speaker. For the series system this means a volume of 4,000 one-page exercises, with 25 sentences per exercise. Altogether there would be 100,000 sentences. This is comparable to my calculation that a junior high student has a vocabulary of more than 100,000 words.

The Foreign Service Institute of the Department of State is more conservative in its estimate of time requirements for foreign language achievement. To obtain the level of S-3, R-3 (Minimum professional proficiency), their students of average aptitude will take 1000 to 1200 hours (6 to 7 months of intensive study). That is for languages in the Germanic and Romance families. Slavic languages take 15 months (2625 hours); most other languages, 18 months (3150 hours); Amharic, Arabic, Chinese, Japanese, and Korean take 25 months of intensive study (4375 hours) (Wilds 1962).

In an ordinary school year of 180 days, at one hour a day it would take five years to reach 900 hours of instruction in a foreign language. We can safely conclude that a student cannot become bilingual in less than five years of study, one hour a day.

In practice, very few students are bilingual after five years of study. One reason is that language learning requires a certain concentration of effort. It does not help to dilute this study to less than one hour a day and to drop language study altogether for the summer months. Gouin baldly states that, "In point of fact, whoever does not, within the space of the four seasons of one year, manage to learn practically all there is to be learnt of the basis of a language, will never learn it" (Gouin 1880, 298). "Never" is too strong a word; there is always a new chance next year. But every year a large part of last year's diluted study will have to be relearned. And if the native speaker keeps learning his own language at the average rate of 10,000 words a year during the first twenty years, the foreign language student who learns less will always be getting farther and farther behind his age level.[20]

But there is another reason why 900 hours spread over five years is not enough. The attempt is rarely made to teach the students the huge vocabulary that is necessary to translate the student's individuality into the foreign language. With the grammar-translation method, the student might learn only 5,000 words in five years—one twentieth of what he would need. Except for Gouin, other methods are not very much more ambitious. Gouin was one of the very few language teachers to devise a program for systematic study of the language above the elementary level. The common practice of having advanced college courses in "conversation" and other advanced courses in "literature" is not adequate for mastery of a language. Important large domains of language are left out this way. A five or six year high school curriculum would have the flexibility to study all important domains of

[20] It is not clear, however, what the optimum number of hours per day is for foreign language study. The Foreign Service Institute estimates that it takes fewer hours of study to learn a language if the study is part time (one hour of class and one of study every day) than if it is full time (eight hours a day of class, lab, and study) (Wilds 1962). But these part-time students are all Foreign Service officers stationed overseas, and they have a certain amount of contact with the language outside their study time. My experience would indicate that full-time study is usually more effective. But one hour a day is probably intensive enough to be effective in most situations if the instruction is good.

vocabulary without the worry of whether or not it was being scholarly. A wide range of study is necessary for bilingualism —study of journalism, popular sciences, the arts, and politics as well as literature. The advanced levels of language study and the processes of perfecting a language are in serious need of re-evaluation and further study.

Language study which is not broadly conceived will often lead to a kind of pseudo-bilingualism. The pseudo-bilingual might be able to carry on his daily affairs in his foreign language, and to prattle on about this and that, but still be unable to catch the subtleties of the language or to understand things outside his narrow domain of experience. Erik Erikson has pointed out how the rulers of colonial territories often believe that their subjects are inherent liars, when in fact these subjects are just pseudo-bilinguals (Erikson 1969, 259). I have tested an Indian who came to this country to teach biology in high school. He had studied English for fifteen years in Bombay, and refused to admit that he had any problem other than his Indian accent. But on a standardized reading test for native speakers, he was below scale for tenth grade (i.e., lower than the lowest expected scores). Another case was a highly placed Vietnamese who even after a year in this country was able to read only as well as the bottom 5 per cent of high school seniors. Yet both of these men were glib in their conversation (though difficult to understand) and they were trying to carry on their affairs in English.

It is not at all impossible to become bilingual, however. And there are several encouraging trends in American education which should help us produce bilinguals in a way we have never been able to do before. For one thing, more and more students are able to study a foreign language for four years or more before entering college. If students could spend an hour a day on a foreign language beginning in seventh grade, they would have time to become very good in the language before completing high school. Foreign language instruction in the elementary schools might have potential, too, but if less than an hour a day is spent on language, and if the study is not serious, then it might as well be dropped from the elementary school curriculum (cf. Page 1966). The increase in intensive summer schools and foreign language camps for both high school and college is a very important trend to be encouraged. If this intensive study can be done overseas, so much the better. For language majors, the junior year abroad is almost essential.

In 1965 only the top 10 to 25 per cent of language majors reached the level of full professional proficiency in their foreign language (Carroll 1967). This should actually be the goal of many others who are not even language majors —especially anyone who plans to go on for graduate study. It is a realistic goal, a goal adopted and reached by many Europeans in learning English.

There are two requirements for us if we want to make our language teaching goal the production of bilinguals. First, we must provide adequate time. But more important, we must have high quality instruction using methods which are adequate to the task.

REFERENCES

Allen, Harold B., ed. *Applied English Linguistics*. New York: Appleton-Century-Crofts, 1958.

Allen, Harold B., ed. *Teaching English as a Second Language*. New York: McGraw-Hill, 1965a.

Allen, Harold B. "Face East When Facing Non-English Speakers." 1965b. In V. F. Allen 1965.

Allen, Virginia French, ed. *On Teaching English to Speakers of Other Languages, Series One*. Papers read at the TESOL conference, Tucson, Arizona, May, 1964. Champaign, Illinois: National Council of Teachers of English, 1965.

Anthony, Edward M. "Approach, method, and technique." *English Language Teaching*, XVII (1963), 63-67. Reprinted in H. B. Allen 1965a.

Bandura, A. and R. H. Walters. *Social Learning and Personality Development*. New York: Holt, 1965.

Barall, Milton. "The Contribution of Emile Blais de Sauzé to the Teaching of Modern Foreign Languages." Unpublished doctoral dissertation. New York University, 1949.

Bauer, Camille, Margaret D. Barton, Patricia O'Connor. *Le Français: Lire, Parler, et Ecrire*. New York: Holt, 1964a.

Bauer, Camille, Margaret D. Barton, Patricia O'Connor. *Teachers' Manual for Le Français: Lire, Parler, et Ecrire*. New York: Holt, 1964b.

107

Belasco, Simon, and Albert Valdman. *College French in the New Key*. Boston: Heath, 1965.

Berko, Jean. "The Child's Learning of English Morphology." *Word*, XIV (1958), 150-177.

Berlitz Publications Staff. *English: First Book*. New York: Berlitz Publications, 1967.

Berlitz, M. D. *Methode Berlitz*. New York: Berlitz and Co., 1887.

Berlitz, M. D. *French, with or without a Master*. New York: Berlitz and Co., 1891.

Berlitz, M. D. *Verb Drill*. New York: Berlitz and Co., 1893.

Berlitz, M. D. *Deuxième Livre*. New York: Berlitz and Co., 1905.

Berlitz, M. D. *Le Genre des Substantifs*. New York: Berlitz and Co., 1917a.

Berlitz, M. D. *Key to the First French Book*. New York: Berlitz and Co., 1917b.

Bétis, Victor, and Howard Swan. *The Facts of Life*. London: Philip, 1896a.

Bétis, Victor, and Howard Swan. *Class-room Conversations in French*. New York: Scribner, 1896b.

Black, Max. *Models and Metaphors: Studies in Language and Philosophy*. Ithaca, N.Y.: Cornell University Press, 1962.

Bloomfield, Leonard. *An Introduction to the Study of Language*. New York: Holt, 1914.

Bloomfield, Leonard. *Language*. New York: Holt, 1933.

Bloomfield, Leonard. *Outline Guide for the Practical Study of Foreign Languages*. Baltimore: Linguistic Society of America, 1942.

Bloomfield, Leonard. *Colloquial Dutch*. New York: Holt, 1944.

Bloomfield, Leonard, Luba Petrova, and I. M. Lesnin. *Spoken Russian*. New York: Holt, 1945.

Bolinger, Dwight L. et al. *Modern Spanish: A Project of the Modern Language Association*. New York: Harcourt, 1960; 2nd ed., 1966.

Bolinger, Dwight L. et al. *Instructor's Manual, revised, for Modern Spanish*. New York: Harcourt, 1963.

Bolling, George Melville. "Acceleration of Language Teaching and the Classics." *Classical Philology*, XXXIX:2 (1944), 101-106.

Bowen, J. Donald, and Robert P. Stockwell. "Foreword to Modern English," 1968 (Rutherford 1968).

"Brainwashing to Teach," *Time Magazine*, LXXXIX:7 (February 17, 1967), 63-64.

Brekke, K. "Indberetning om en hosten 1893 foretagen stipendiereise til England for at studere Gouins metode for undervisning i sprog." *Universitets- og skole-annaler*, IX:1-3 (1894), 18-79.

Brooks, Nelson. *Language and Language Learning*. New York: Harcourt, 1964.

Carroll, John B., and Stanley M. Sapon. *Modern Language Aptitude Test, Manual*. New York: The Psychological Corporation, 1959.

Carroll, John B. "Research on teaching foreign languages." 1963a. In N. L. Gage, ed. *Handbook of Research on Teaching*. Chicago: Rand McNally, 1963.

Carroll, John B. *Programmed Self-instruction in Mandarin Chinese*. Wellesley, Mass.: Language Testing Fund, 1963b.

Carroll, John B. "A Primer of Programmed Instruction in Foreign Language Teaching," *IRAL*, I:2 (1963c), 115-141.

Carroll, John B. "The Contributions of Psychological Theory and Educational Research to the Teaching of Foreign Languages," *Modern Language Journal* V, (1965) 273-281.

Carroll, John B. "Research in language teaching: the last five years." Reports of the Working Committees, Northeast Conference on the Teaching of Foreign Languages. New York: MLA Materials Center, 1966.

Carroll, John B. "The Foreign Language Attainments of Language Majors in the Senior Year." Cambridge: Harvard University, 1967 (available from ERIC Document Reproduction Service).

Carroll, John B. "What Does the Pennsylvania Foreign Language Research Project Tell Us?" *Foreign Language Annals*, III:2 (1969), 214-236.

Chao, Yuen Ren. *Mandarin Primer*. Cambridge: Harvard, 1961.

Cherubini, G., and V. E. Condon. *Curso Practico de Español para Principiantes*. Philadelphia: Winston, 1931.

Chesnutt, H. M., M. W. Olivenbaum, and N. F. Rosebaugh. *The Road to Latin*. Philadelphia: Winston, 1932.

Chomsky, Carol. *The Acquisition of Syntax in Children from 5 to 10*. Cambridge, Mass.: M.I.T. Press, 1969.

Chomsky, Noam. *Syntactic Structures*. The Hague: Mouton, 1957.

Chomsky, Noam. "A review of B. F. Skinner's Verbal Behavior" (Skinner 1957). *Language*, XXXV:1 (1959), 26-58. Reprinted in Fodor and Katz 1964.

Chomsky, Noam. "Current Issues in Linguistic Theory." 1964. In Fodor and Katz 1964.

Chomsky, Noam. *Aspects of the Theory of Syntax*. Cambridge: M.I.T., 1965.

Chomsky, Noam. *Cartesian Linguistics*. New York: Harper & Row, 1966a.

Chomsky, Noam. "Linguistic Theory." Reports of the Working Committees, Northeast Conference on the Teaching of Foreign Languages. New York: MLA Materials Center, 1966b.

Chomsky, Noam, and Morris Halle. *Sound Patterns of English*. New York: Harper & Row, 1968.

Coleman, Algernon. *The Teaching of Modern Foreign Languages in the United States*. New York: Macmillan, 1929.

Côté, Dominique G., Sylvia Narius Levy, and Patricia O'Connor. *Le Français: Ecouter et Parler, Teachers' Edition*. New York: Holt, 1962.

Dacanay, Fe R. *Techniques and Procedures in Second Language Teaching*. Quezon City: Phoenix Publishing House, 1963.

DeCamp, David. *Linguistics and Teaching Foreign Languages*. Chapter 13 of Linguistics Today, A. A. Hill, ed. New York: Basic Books, 1969.

de Sauzé, Emile B. *Cours Pratique de Français pour Commençants*. Philadelphia: Winston, 1919.

de Sauzé, Emile B., and Harriet M. True. *Grammaire Française*. Philadelphia: Winston, 1920.

de Sauzé, Emile B. *Exercises on French Irregular Verbs, and Verb Blanks*. New York: Holt, 1922.

de Sauzé, Emile B., ed. *Contes Gais*. Philadelphia: Winston, 1924.

de Sauzé, Emile B., ed. *Sept Comedies Modernes*. New York: Holt, 1925.

de Sauzé, Emile B. "A Pedagogical and Psychological Basis for a First-year Latin Course," *Classical Journal*, XXI (1926).

de Sauzé, Emile B. *The Cleveland Plan for the Teaching of Modern Languages with Special Reference to French*. Philadelphia: Winston, 1929; rev. ed. 1959. This book was also issued with special reference to other languages.

de Sauzé, Emile B., ed. *Jean Valjean—extrait des Miserables de Victor Hugo*. New York: Holt, 1930.

de Sauzé, Emile B., ed. *Lisons Donc*. New York: Holt, 1932.

de Sauzé, Emile B., and V. E. Condon. *Spanish Practice Book—First Year*. St. Louis: Webster, 1932.

de Sauzé, Emile B., and W. L. Connor. "Notes on Some Phases of Foreign Language Instruction in Cleveland." *Education,* LV (1934), 1-5.

de Sauzé, Emile B. *Nouvelles Aventures de d'Artagnan.* New York: Holt, 1935.

de Sauzé, Emile B., and W. W. du Breuil. *Cahier d'exercises: a Workbook to Accompany Cours Pratique de Français.* Philadelphia: Winston, 1936.

de Sauzé, Emile B., and Agnes M. Dureau. *Un Peu de Tout.* Philadelphia: Winston, 1937.

de Sauzé, Emile B., and Agnes M. Dureau. *Commençons à Lire.* New York: Holt, 1940.

de Sauzé, Emile B. "Unit in 'Intensive' Reading," *Modern Language Journal,* XXIX:4(1945a), 260-269.

de Sauzé, Emile B. "L'Enseignement des langues estrangères par la radio dans les écoles de Cleveland," *French Review,* XIX:2(1945b), 101-102.

de Sauzé, Emile B. *Nouveau Cours Pratique de Français pour Commençants.* Philadelphia: Winston, 1946.

de Sauzé, Emile B. 1959. See de Sauzé 1929.

de Sauzé, Emile B. General editor of Lensner (1928), Cherubini and Condon (1931), and Chesnutt et al. (1932).

Diller, Karl C. " 'Compound' and 'Coordinate' Bilingualism—a Conceptual Artifact." *Word.* In Press.

Diller, Karl C. " 'Resonance' and Language Learning." *Linguistics.* In Press.

Erikson, Erik H. *Gandhi's Truth.* New York: Norton, 1969.

Ferguson, Charles. *Linguistic Theory and Language Learning.* Washington: Georgetown Monograph Series 16, 115-124, 1963.

Ferguson, Charles. *Applied Linguistics.* Reports of the working committees, Northeast Conference on the Teaching of Foreign Languages. New York: MLA Materials Center, 1966.

Fodor, Jerry A., and Jerrold J. Katz. *The Structure of Language: Readings in the Philosophy of Language.* Englewood Cliffs, N.J.: Prentice-Hall, 1964.

Fries, Charles C. *Teaching and Learning English as a Foreign Language.* Ann Arbor: The University of Michigan Press, 1945.

Fries, Charles C., and Yao Shen. *An Intensive Course in English for Chinese Students.* Ann Arbor: English Language Institute, University of Michigan, 1946.

Fries, Charles C. "A New Approach to Language Learning." Tokyo: ELEC Publications 4, (1960) 1-4. Reprinted in H. B. Allen (1965).

Fries, Charles C. "The Bloomfield 'School.' " In Mohrmann et al. (1961).

Gage, W. W. *Contrastive Studies in Linguistics.* Washington, D.C.: Center for Applied Linguistics, 1961.

Gatenby, E. V. "Conditions for Success in Language Learning," *English Language Teaching*, VI (1950), 143-150. Reprinted in H. B. Allen 1965.

Gouin, François. *L'art d'enseigner et d'étudier les langues.* Paris: Librairie Fischbacher, 1880. Page references are to the translation by Howard Swan and Victor Bétis, *The Art of Teaching and Studying Languages.* London: Philip, 1892.

Gourio, Eugène. *La classe en français.* Boston: Houghton Mifflin, 1920.

Gourio, Eugene. *The Direct Method of Teaching French.* Boston: Houghton Mifflin, 1921.

Graves, Mortimer. "Languages in American Education." Mimeographed, 1963.

Haas, Mary R. "The Linguist as a Teacher of Languages, " *Language*, XIX (1943), 203-208.

Haas, Mary R. "The Application of Linguistics to Language Teaching." In A. L. Kroeber, ed. *Anthropology Today.* Chicago: University of Chicago Press, 1953.

Hall, Robert A., Jr. *Leave Your Language Alone!* Ithaca, N.Y.: Linguistica, 1950.

Hall, Robert A., Jr. *Hands Off Pidgin English!* Sydney: Pacific Publications, 1955.

Hall, Robert A., Jr. *New Ways to Learn a Foreign Language: The New Linguistic Way That Has Revolutionized Language Learning.* New York: Bantam, 1966.

Halle, Morris. "Phonology in Generative Grammar," *Word*, XVIII (1962), 54-72. Reprinted in Fodor and Katz, 1964.

Halle, Morris. "On the Bases of Phonology." In Fodor and Katz, 1964. This is a revised version of "Questions of Linguistics," Il Nuovo Cimento, XIII, Series X (1958), 494-517.

Halle, Morris, and Kenneth N. Stevens. "Speech Recognition: A Model and a Program for Research." In Fodor and Katz, 1964.

Hammer, John H. *A Bibliography of Contrastive Linguistics.* Washington, D.C.: Center for Applied Linguistics, 1965.

Hanson, Norwood Russell. *Patterns of Discovery.* London: Cambridge University Press, 1958.

Harvey, Philip R., "Minimal Passing Scores on the Graduate

School Foreign Language Tests." *Foreign Languages Annals*, II:2 (1968), 165-173.

Haugen, Einar. *Spoken Norwegian*. New York: Holt, 1947.

Haugen, Einar. "From Army Camp to Classroom: The Story of an Elementary Language Text," *Scandinavian Studies* (1951), 138-151.

Haugen, Einar. "Linguists and the Wartime Program of Language Teaching," Modern Language Journal, XXXIX (1955), 243-245.

Haugen, Einar. "Bilingualism as a Goal in Foreign Language Teaching." In V. F. Allen, 1965.

Heness, Gottlieb. *Der Leitfaden für den Unterricht in der deütschen Sprache, ohne Sprachlehre und Wörterbuch*. 2nd Edition, with an introduction in English. Boston: Schönhof und Möller, 1875.

Hill, Archibald A. "Grammaticality," *Word*, XVII (1961), 1-10.

Hockett, Charles F. *A Course in Modern Linguistics*. New York: Macmillan, 1958.

Hockett, Charles F. "The Foundations of Language in Man, the Small-mouthed Animal (a review of Lenneberg 1967). Scientific American (Nov. 1967), 140-144.

Hockett, Charles F. *The State of the Art*. The Hague: Mouton, 1968.

Householder, F. W. A review of Hockett 1968. *Journal of Linguistics*, VI:1 (1970), 129-134.

Hydén, Holger. "The Biochemical Aspects of Learning and Memory." Public lecture at Harvard University, 9 February 1967.

Jakobovits, Leon A. *Foreign Language Learning: A Psycholinguistic Analysis of the Issues*. Rowley, Mass.: Newbury House, 1970.

Jespersen, Otto. *How to Teach a Foreign Language*. Translated by Sophia Yhlen-Olsen Bertelsen. London: G. Allen, 1904.

Jespersen, Otto. *Language, Its Nature, Development, and Origin*. London: G. Allen, 1922.

Joos, Martin. *Readings in Linguistics: The Development of Descriptive Linguistics in America Since 1925*. New York: American Council of Learned Societies, 1958.

Joos, Martin "Linguistic Prospects in the United States." In Mohrmann et al., 1961.

Keesee, Elizabeth, Gregory G. La Grone, Patricia O'Connor. *Español: Leer, Hablar y Escribir*. New York: Holt, 1964.

Kuhn, Thomas S. *The Structure of Scientific Revolutions*. Chicago: The University of Chicago Press, 1962.

Lado, Robert. *Linguistics Across Cultures*. Ann Arbor: The University of Michigan Press, 1957.

Lado, Robert, and Charles C. Fries. *An Intensive Course in English*. 4 vols. Ann Arbor: The University of Michigan Press, 1958.

Lado, Robert. *Language Teaching: A Scientific Approach*. New York: McGraw Hill, 1964.

La Grone, Gregory G., Andrea Sendón McHenry, Patricia O'Connor. *Español: Hablar Y Leer*. New York: Holt, 1962.

Lénard, Yvone, and Ralph M. Hester. *L'art de la conversation*. New York: Harper & Row, 1967.

Lénard, Yvone, ed. *Le matin des magiciens*, by Louis Pauwels et Jacques Bergier, New York: Harper & Row, 1967.

Lénard, Yvone. *Parole et Pensee*. New York: Harper & Row, 1965.

Lénard, Yvone. *Jeunes voix, jeunes visages*. New York: Harper & Row, 1969.

Lenneberg, Eric H. *New Directions on the Study of Language*. Cambridge, Mass.: MIT, 1964.

Lenneberg, Eric H. *Biological Foundations of Language*. New York: Wiley, 1967.

Lensner, Herman J. *Neuer praktischer Lehrgang*. New York: Holt, 1928.

Lensner, Herman J. "The Cleveland Experiment." Modern Language Journal, XIII (1929), 393-398.

Lester, Mark. *Readings in Applied Transformational Grammar*. New York: Holt, 1970.

Marks, E. *L'Enseignement des Langues d'après le Cleveland Plan*. Montpellier, France: Imprimerie du *Progrès*, 1933.

Mathieu, Gustave. "Pitfalls of pattern practice," an exegesis. *Modern Language Journal*, XLVIII (1964), 20-24.

McClain, William H. "Twenty-fifth anniversary of the Cleveland Plan." Reprinted in M. Newmark, 1948.

McKinnon, Kenneth Richard. "An Experimental Study of the Learning of Syntax in Second Language Learning." Cambridge: Harvard University Ed.D. dissertation, 1965.

Méras, E. A. "Some Remarks on the Interpretation of the Coleman Report," *French Review*, IV (1931), 311-318.

Mercier, Louis J. A. et al. "A Statement of Principles for the Integration of the Development of Modern Foreign Language Abilities versus the Basic Recommendations of the Coleman Report," *Modern Language Journal*, XV (1931), 619-628.

Miller, George A. "Some Psychological Studies of Grammar," *American Psychologist*, XVII:11 (1962), 748-766.

Miller, George A. "Language and psychology." 1964a. In Lenneberg 1964.

Miller, George A. "The Psycholinguists." 1964b. Appendix to Osgood and Sebeok 1965.

Modern Language Association. *Selective List of Materials*. New York: Modern Language Association, 1962.

Mohrmann, Christine, Alf Sommerfelt, and Joshua Whatmough. *Trends in European and American Linguistics 1930-1960*. Utrecht: Spectrum Publishers, 1961.

Morgan, B. Q. "The Coleman Report and the Reading Method," Modern Language Journal, XIV (1930), 618-623.

Moulton, William G. "The Cornell Language Program," *PMLA*, LXVII, 6 (1952), 38-46.

Moulton, William G. "Linguistics and Language Teaching in the United States 1940-1960." In Mohrmann et al. 1961.

Mueller, Theodore H., and Ralph R. Leutenegger. "Some Inferences about an Intensified Oral Approach to the Teaching of French Based on a Study of Course Dropouts," *Modern Language Journal*, XLVIII:2 (1964), 91-94.

Mulhauser, Ruth. "Experiment or Tradition?" *Modern Language Journal*, XL (1956), 462-464.

Newmark, Leonard. "Grammatical Theory and Teaching English as a Foreign Language," *The 1963 Conference Papers of the English Language Section of the National Association of Foreign Student Affairs*, NAFSA, New York, 1964. Reprinted in Lester, 1970.

Newmark, Leonard. "How Not to Interfere with Language Learning." IJAL, XXXII:12 (1966). Reprinted in Lester, 1970.

Newmark, Leonard. "How Not to Interfere with Language Learning." In *Najam* 1966.

Newmark, Leonard. *Notes on the Study of Language Acquisition*. Actes du Xe Congrès International de Linguistes, III: 245-250. Bucarest: Editions de L'académie de la république socialiste de Roumanie, 1967.

Newmark, Leonard, and David A. Reibel. *Necessity and Sufficiency in Language Learning*. IRAL IV:2 (1968), 145-164. Reprinted in Lester, 1970.

Newmark, Maxim ed. *Twentieth Century Modern Language Teaching* New York: The Philosophical Library, 1948.

Nida, Eugene A. "Some Psychological Problems in Second Language Learning," *Language Learning*, VIII, 1 (1958), 7-15. Reprinted in H. B. Allen 1965a.

O'Connor, Patricia, and W. F. Twaddell. "Intensive Training for an Oral Approach in Language Teaching," *Modern Language Journal*, XLIV:2 (1960), 2.

O'Neil, Wayne A. "The Reality of Grammars: Some Literary Evidence." Paper presented to the Linguistic Circle of New York, 1966.

Osgood, Charles E., and Thomas A. Sebeok. *Psycholinguistics*. Bloomington: Indiana University Press, 1965.

Page, Mary M. "We Dropped FLES," *Modern Language Journal*, L:3 (1966), 139-141.

Palmer, Harold E. *One Hundred Substitution Tables*. (Colloquial English, Part I). Cambridge, England: Heffer, 1916.

Palmer, Harold E. *The Scientific Study and Teaching of Languages*. Yonkers, N.Y.: World, 1917.

Palmer, Harold E. *The Principles of Language Study*. Yonkers, N.Y.: World, 1921.

Palmer, Harold E. *English Intonation with Systematic Exercises*. Cambridge, England: Heffer, 1922.

Palmer, Harold E. *A Grammar of Spoken English on a Strictly Phonetic Basis*. Cambridge, England: Heffer, 1924.

Penfield, Wilder. "A Consideration of the Neuro Physiological Mechanism of Speech and Some Educational Consequences," *Proceedings of the American Academy of Arts and Sciences*, LXXXII, (1953), 201-214.

Penfield, Wilder. "The Uncommitted Cortex," Atlantic Monthly, CCXIV:1 (1964), 77-91.

Pfister, Franz J. *Deutsch durch Deutsch*. New York: Harper & Row, 1968.

Politzer, Robert L. *Teaching French: An Introduction to Applied Linguistics*. Boston: Ginn, 1960.

Pucciani, Oreste F., and Jacqueline Hamel. *Langue et Langage*. New York: Holt, 1967.

Rehder, Helmut, Ursula Thomas, W. Freeman Twaddell, and Patricia O'Connor. *Deutsch: Verstehen und Sprechen; Teacher's Edition*. New York: Holt, 1962a.

Rehder, Helmut, Ursula Thomas, W. Freeman Twaddell, and Patricia O'Connor. *Ubungsbuch*. New York: Holt, 1962b.

Rehder, Helmut, Ursula Thomas, W. Freeman Twaddell, and Patricia O'Connor. *Deutsch:Sprechen und Lesen*. New York: Holt, 1963a.

Rehder, Helmut, Ursula Thomas, W. Freeman Twaddell, and Patricia O'Connor. *Complete Classroom Manual for use with Deutsch: Sprechen und Lesen*. New York: Holt, 1963b.

Rehder, Helmut, Ursula Thomas, and W. Freeman Twaddell. *Deutsch: Lesen und Denken*. New York: Holt, 1964.

Rehder, Helmut, Ursula Thomas, and W. Freeman Twaddell. *Tapescript to Accompany Deutsch: Lesen und Denken.* New York: Holt, 1965.

Rehder, Helmut, Ursula Thomas, W. Freeman Twaddell, and Harry A. Walbruck. *Deutsch: Denken, Wissen, und Kennen.* New York: Holt, 1966.

Reibel, David A. *Language Learning Analysis.* IRAL VII:4, (1969), 283-294.

Rivers, Wilga M. *The Psychologist and the Foreign Language Teacher.* Chicago: The University of Chicago Press, 1964.

Rouse, W. H. D., and R. B. Appleton. *Latin on the Direct Method.* London: University of London Press, Ltd., 1925.

Rutherford, William E. *Modern English.* New York: Harcourt, Brace & World, 1968.

Sapir, Edward. "The Psychological Reality of Phonemes." 1933. In D. Mandelbaum, ed. *The Selected Writings of Edward Sapir.* Berkeley: University of California Press, 1949.

Saporta, Sol. "Applied Linguistics and Generative Grammar." In Valdman 1966.

Saussure, Ferdinand de. *Cours de linguistique générale.* 1915. Publié par Charles Bally et Albert Sechehaye avec la collaboration de Albert Riedlinger. Paris: Payot. Page references to the translation by Wade Baskin, *Course in General Linguistics.* New York: Philosophical Library, 1959.

Sauveur, Lambert. *Introduction to the Teaching of Living Languages without Grammar or Dictionary.* New York: F. W. Christern, 1875.

Sauveur, Lambert. *The Natural Method: Introduction to the Teaching of Ancient Languages.* New York: Holt, 1878.

Scheffler, Israel. *Conditions of Knowledge.* Chicago: Scott, Foresman, 1965.

Skinner, B. F. "The Science of Learning and the Art of Teaching," *Harvard Educational Review,* XXIV (1954), 86-97.

Skinner, B. F. *Verbal Behavior.* New York: Appleton Century Crofts, 1957.

Smith, Philip D., Jr. *A Comparison of the Cognitive and Audiolingual Approaches to Foreign Language Instruction: The Pennsylvania Foreign Language Project.* Philadelphia: The Center for Curriculum Development, Inc., 1970.

Spolsky, Bernard. *A Psycholinguistic Critique of Programmed Foreign Language Instruction.* IRAL IV:2, (1966), 119-129.

Spolsky, Bernard. *The Value of Volunteers in English Language Teaching, Or Why Pay For It When You Can Get It For Nothing.* A paper presented to the National Association of Foreign Student Affairs, San Francisco, 1968.

Spolsky, Bernard. *Linguistics and Language Pedagogy-- Applications or Implications?* Georgetown Monograph Series on Languages and Linguistics, Number 22, (1969), 143-145.

Stern, H. H. *Foreign Languages in Primary Education.* Hamburg: UNESCO Institute for Education, 1963.

Stieglitz, Gerhard. *The Berlitz Method,* Modern Language Journal 39:6, (1955), 300-310.

Sweet, Henry. *The Practical Study of Languages.* London: Oxford University Press, 1899.

Sweet, Waldo. *Latin: A Structural Appraoch.* Ann Arbor: The University of Michigan Press, 1957.

Teeter, Karl V. "Descriptive Linguistics in America: Triviality vs. Irrelevance," *Word*, XX:2 (1964), 197-206.

Traversa, Vincenz. *Parola e Pensiero.* New York: Harper & Row, 1967.

Twaddell, W. Freeman. *On Defining the Phoneme.* Language Monograph No. 166 (1935). Reprinted in Joos, 1958.

Twaddell, W. Freeman. "Meanings, Habits, and Rules," *Education*, XLIX (1948).

Twaddell, W. Freeman. *Foreign Language Instruction at the Second Level.* New York: Holt, 1963.

Twaddell, W. Freeman, Robert Brooks, Frederick D. Eddy, Judy Franklin, Elizabeth Keesee, Elizabeth Michael, and Patricia O'Connor. *Introducing Spanish.* New York: Holt, 1964a.

Twaddell, W. Freeman, Robert Brooks, Frederick D. Eddy, Judy Franklin, Elizabeth Keesee, Elizabeth Michael, and Patricia O'Connor. *Teacher's Manual for Introducing Spanish.* New York: Holt, 1964b.

Twaddell, W. Freeman, Robert Brooks, Frederick D. Eddy, Judy Franklin, Elizabeth Keesee, Elizabeth Michael, and Patricia O'Connor. *Teacher's Manual for Primer Curso.* New York: Holt, 1964c.

Twaddell, W. Freeman. See O'Connor and Twaddell 1960; Rehder et al. 1962a, 1962b, 1966a, 1963b, 1964, 1965, 1966. In addition, Twaddell is general editorial advisor for Côté et al. 1962; La Grone et al. 1962; Keesee et al. 1964; and Bauer et al. 1964a, 1964b.

Valdman, Albert. "Toward Self-instruction in Foreign Language Learning," IRAL, II:1 (1964), 1-36.

Valdman, Albert, ed. *Trends in Language Teaching.* New York: McGraw-Hill, 1966.

Weir, Ruth. *Language in the Crib.* The Hague: Mouton, 1961.

Whatmough, Joshua. "A Review of Bloch and Trager's Outline of Linguistic Analysis" *Classical Philology,* XXXVIII:3 (1943), 210-211.

Whatmough, Joshua. "Up from Gilgal: A Rejoinder," *Classical Philology,* XXXIX:4 (1944), 218-222. A reply to Bolling 1944, which in turn replies to Whatmough 1943.

Whitney, William Dwight. "Steinthal and the Psychological Theory of Language," *North American Review,* XLIV (1872). Reprinted in Whitney 1873.

Whitney, William Dwight. *Oriental and Linguistic Studies.* New York: Scribner, Armstrong, and Co., 1873.

Whitney, William Dwight. *The Life and Growth of Language: An Outline of Linguistic Science.* New York: Appleton, 1875.

Wilds, Claudia P. "Time Requirements for Foreign Language Achievement." Washington, D.C.: The Foreign Service Institute (mimeographed), 1962.

INDEX

A

L

Lado, Robert, 3-6, 9, 19, 40
La Fontaine, 61
La Grone, Gregory G., 46
Lancelot, 51
Lénard, Yvone, 4, 67, 79
Lenneberg, Eric H., 10, 28-30, 32
Leutenegger, Ralph, 16
Lundell, 3

M

Mathieu, Gustave, 49
Meillet, A., 1
Meras, E. A., 4
Mercier, Louis J. A., 4
Miller, George A., 23, 56
Morgan, B. Q., 4
Moulton, William G., 10, 14, 15, 17, 78, 82
Mueller, Theodore H., 16
Mulhauser, Ruth, 77

N

Newmark, Leonard, 83-88

O

O'Connor, Patricia, 9, 25, 47
Ollendorf, 2, 52
O'Neil, Wayne A., vii, 24

P

Page, Mary M., 105
Palmer, Harold E., 3, 4, 5, 9, 40, 42, 45
Penfield, Wilder, 30
Pfister, Franz, 79
Politzer, Robert L., 7
Pucciani, Oreste F., 4, 79

R

Rehder, Helmut, 46-48
Reibel, David A., 85-88
Rivers, Wilga M., 9, 14

Rutherford, William E., 41, 49, 83
Ryle, Gilbert, 26

S

Sapir, Edward, 24
Sapon, Stanley, 93
Saporta, Sol, viii, 81-82
Saussure, Ferdinand de, 11, 12
Sauveur, Lambert, 67
Sayce, 3
Scheffler, Israel, 26
Sievers, 3
Skinner, B. F., 13, 14, 39
Smith, Philip D., 17, 94
Spolsky, Bernard, 83-85
Stieglitz, Gerhard, 71
Stockwell, Robert P., 49
Storm, 3
Sturtevant, E., 1
Sweet, Henry, 3
Sweet, Waldo, 20

T

Teeter, Karl V., vii 19
Traversa, Vincenzo, 79
True, Harriet M., 74
Twaddell, W. Freeman, 9, 11, 15, 25, 26, 36, 45-47, 49, 83

U

Ustinov, Peter, 31

V

Valdman, Albert, 5, 39, 48
Vergil, 61
Vietor, W., 3

W

Watkins, Calvert, vii
Weir, Ruth, 29
Whatmough, Joshua, 20
Whitney, William Dwight, 13
Wilds, Claudia P., 93, 103, 104